Cases in
Operations
Management

Cases in
Operations
Management

Fourth Edition

Selected cases from:

Operations and Process Management: Principles and Practice for Strategic Impact
Third Edition
Nigel Slack, Alistair Brandon-Jones, Robert Johnston & Alan Betts

Cases in Operations Management
Third Edition
Robert Johnston, Stuart Chambers, Christine Harland, Alan Harrison and Nigel Slack

Operations Management
Sixth Edition
Nigel Slack, Stuart Chambers and Robert Johnston

Service Operations Management: Improving Service Delivery
Fourth Edition
Robert Johnston, Graham Clark and Michael Shulver

Operations Management
Seventh Edition
Nigel Slack, Alistair Brandon-Jones and Robert Johnston

PEARSON

Harlow, England • London • New York • Boston • San Francisco • Toronto • Sydney • Auckland • Singapore • Hong Kong
Tokyo • Seoul • Taipei • New Delhi • Cape Town • Sao Paulo • Mexico City • Madrid • Amsterdam • Munich • Paris • Milan

Pearson Education Limited
Edinburgh Gate
Harlow
Essex CM20 2JE

And associated companies throughout the world

Visit us on the World Wide Web at:
www.pearson.com/uk

First published 2007
This edition © Pearson Education Limited 2014

Compiled from:

Operations and Process Management: Principles and Practice for Strategic Impact
Third Edition
Nigel Slack, Alistair Brandon-Jones, Robert Johnston & Alan Betts
ISBN 978 0 273 75187 8
© Pearson Education Limited 2006, 2009, 2012

Cases in Operations Management
Third Edition
Robert Johnston, Stuart Chambers, Christine Harland, Alan Harrison and Nigel Slack
ISBN 978 0 273 65531 2
© Robert Johnston, Stuart Chambers, Christine Harland, Alan Harrison and Nigel Slack 1993, 2003

Operations Management
Sixth Edition
Nigel Slack, Stuart Chambers and Robert Johnston
ISBN 978 0 273 73046 0
© Nigel Slack, Stuart Chambers, Christine Harland, Alan Harrison, Robert Johnston 1995, 1998
© Nigel Slack, Stuart Chambers, and Robert Johnston 2001, 2004, 2007, 2010

Service Operations Management: Improving Service Delivery
Fourth Edition
Robert Johnston, Graham Clark and Michael Shulver
ISBN 978 0 273 74048 3
© Pearson Education Limited 2012

Operations Management
Seventh Edition
Nigel Slack, Alistair Brandon-Jones and Robert Johnston
ISBN 978 0 273 77620 8
© Nigel Slack, Stuart Chambers, Christine Harland, Alan Harrison, Robert Johnston 1995, 1998
© Nigel Slack, Stuart Chambers, Robert Johnston 2001, 2004, 2007, 2010
© Nigel Slack, Alistair Brandon-Jones, Robert Johnston 2013

ISBN 978 1 78376 625 3

Printed and bound in Great Britain by Clays Ltd, Bungay, Suffolk.

Contents

Design House Partnerships at Concept Design Services

'I can't believe how much we have changed in a relatively short time. From being an inward looking manufacturer, we became a customer focused "design and make" operation. Now we are an "integrated service provider". Most of our new business comes from the partnerships we have formed with design houses. In effect, we design products jointly with specialist design houses that have a well-known brand, and offer them a complete service of manufacturing and distribution. In many ways we are now a "business-to-business" company rather than a "business-to-consumer" company.' (Jim Thompson, CEO, Concept Design Services (CDS))

Concept Design Services (CDS) had become one of Europe's most profitable homeware businesses. It had moved in two stages from making precision plastic components, mainly in the aerospace sector, together with some cheap 'homeware' items such as buckets and dustpans, sold under the 'Focus' brand name, to making very high-quality (expensive) stylish homewares with a high 'design value' for well-known brands.

Source: Yang Yu/Alamy Images

The first stage – from 'Focus' to 'Concept'

The initial move into higher margin homeware had been masterminded by Linda Fleet, CDS's Marketing Director. *'My previous experience in the decorative products industry had taught me the importance of fashion and product development, even in mundane products such as paint. Premium-priced colours and new textures would catch the popular imagination and would need supporting by promotion and editorial features in lifestyle magazines. The players who embraced this fashion element of the market were dramatically more profitable than those who simply provided standard ranges. Instinctively, I felt that this must also apply to homeware. We decided to develop a whole coordinated range of such items, and to open up a new distribution network for them to serve the more exclusive stores, kitchen equipment and specialty retailers. Within a year of launching our first new range of kitchen homeware under the 'Concept' brand name, we had over 3,000 retail outlets across Northern Europe with full point-of-sale display facilities and supported by press coverage and product placement on TV 'lifestyle'*

programmes. Within two years 'Concept' products were providing over 75 per cent of our revenue and 90 per cent of our profits.' (The margin on Concept products is many times higher than for the Focus range. During this period the Focus (basic) range continued to be produced, but as a drastically reduced range.)

The second stage – from 'Concept' to 'design house partnerships'

Linda was also the driving force behind the move to design house partnerships. *'It started as a simple design collaboration between our design team and an Italian "design house".'* (Design houses are creative product designers who may, or may not, own a brand of their own, but rarely manufacture or distribute their products, relying on outsourcing to subcontractors.) *'It seemed a natural progression to them asking us to first manufacture and then distribute this and other of their designs. Over the next five years, we built up this business, so now we design (often jointly with the design house), manufacture and distribute products for several of the more prestigious European design houses. We think this sort of business is likely to grow. The design houses appreciate our ability to offer a full service. We can design products in conjunction with their own design staff and offer them a level of manufacturing expertise they can't get elsewhere. More significantly, we can offer a distribution service which is tailored to their needs. From the customer's point of view the distribution arrangements appear to belong to the design house itself. In fact they are based exclusively on our own call centre, warehouse and distribution resources.'*

The most successful collaboration was with Villessi, the Italian designers. Generally it was CDS's design expertise which was attractive to 'design house' partners. Not only did CDS employ professionally respected designers, they had also acquired a reputation for being able to translate difficult technical designs into manufacturable and saleable products. Design house partnerships usually involved relatively long lead times but produced unique products with very high margins, nearly always carrying the design house's brand.

Manufacturing operations

All manufacturing was carried out in a facility located 20 km from Head Office. Its moulding area housed large injection-moulding machines, most with robotic material handling capabilities. Products and components passed to the packing hall, where they were assembled and inspected. The newer more complex products often had to move from moulding to assembly and then back again for further moulding. All products followed the same broad process route but with more products needing several progressive moulding and assembly stages, there was an increase in 'process flow recycling' which was adding complexity. One idea was to devote a separate cell to the newer and more complex products until they had 'bedded in'. This cell could also be used for testing new moulds. However, it would need investment in extra capacity that would not always be fully utilised. After manufacture, products were packed and stored in the adjacent distribution centre.

'When we moved into making the higher margin 'Concept' products, we disposed of most of our older, small injection-moulding machines. Having all larger machines allowed us to use large multi-cavity moulds. This increased productivity by allowing us to produce several products, or components, each machine cycle. It also allowed us to use high-quality and complex moulds which, although cumbersome and more difficult to change over, were very efficient and gave a very high-quality product. For example, with the same labour we could make three items per minute on the old machines, and 18 items per minute on the modern ones using multi-moulds. That's a 600 per cent increase in productivity. We also achieved high-dimensional accuracy, excellent surface finish and extreme consistency of colour. We could do this because of our expertise derived from years making aerospace products. Also, by standardising on single large machines, any mould could fit any machine. This was an ideal situation from a planning perspective, as we were often asked to make small runs of Concept products at short notice.' (Grant Williams, CDS Operations Manager)

Increasing volume and a desire to reduce cost had resulted in CDS subcontracting much (but not all) of its Focus products to other (usually smaller) moulding companies. 'We would never do it with any complex or design house partner products, but it should allow us to reduce the cost of making basic products while releasing capacity for higher margin ones. However there have been quite a few "teething problems". Coordinating the production schedules is currently a problem, as is agreeing quality standards. To some extent it's our own fault. We didn't realise that subcontracting was a skill in its own right. And although we have got over some of the problems, we still do not have a satisfactory relationship with all of our subcontractors.' (Grant Williams, CDS Operations Manager)

Planning and distribution services

The distribution services department of the company was regarded as being at the heart of the company's customer service drive. Its purpose was to integrate the efforts of design, manufacturing and sales by planning the flow of products from production, through the distribution centre, to the customer. Sandra White, the Planning Manager, reported to Linda Fleet and was responsible for the scheduling of all manufacturing and distribution, and for maintaining inventory levels for all the warehoused items. 'We try to stick to a preferred production sequence for each machine and mould so as to minimise set-up times by starting on a light colour, and progressing through a sequence to the darkest. We can change colours in 15 minutes, but because our moulds are large and technically complex, mould changes can take up to three hours. Good scheduling is important to maintain high plant utilisation. With a higher variety of complex products, batch sizes have reduced and it has brought down average utilisation. Often we can't stick to schedules. Short-term changes are inevitable in a fashion market. Certainly better forecasts would help . . . but even our own promotions are sometimes organised at such short notice that we often get caught with stockouts. New products in particular are difficult to forecast, especially when they are 'fashion' items and/or seasonal. Also, I have to schedule production time for new product mould trials; we normally allow 24 hours for the testing of each new mould received, and this has to be done on production machines. Even if we have urgent orders, the needs of the designers always have priority.' (Sandra White)

Customer orders for Concept and design house partnership products were taken by the company's sales call centre located next to the warehouse. The individual orders would then be dispatched using the company's own fleet of medium and small distribution vehicles for UK orders, but using carriers for the Continental European market. A standard delivery timetable was used and an 'express delivery' service was offered for those customers prepared to pay a small delivery premium. However, a recent study had shown that almost 40 per cent of express deliveries were initiated by the company rather than customers. Typically this would be to fulfil deliveries of orders containing products out of stock at the time of ordering. The express delivery service was not required for Focus products because almost all deliveries were to five large customers. The size of each order was usually very large, with deliveries to customers' own distribution depots. However, although the organisation of Focus delivery was relatively straightforward, the consequences of failure were large. Missing a delivery meant upsetting a large customer.

Challenges for CDS

Although the company was financially successful and very well regarded in the homeware industry, there were a number of issues and challenges that it knew it would have to address. The first was the role of the design department and its influence over new product development. New product development had become particularly important to CDS, especially since they had formed alliances with design houses. This had led to substantial growth in both the size and the influence of the design department, which reported to Linda Fleet. *'Building up and retaining design expertise will be the key to our future. Most of our growth is going to come from the business which will be bought in through the creativity and flair of our designers. Those who can combine creativity with an understanding of our partners' business and design needs can now bring in substantial contracts. The existing business is important of course, but growth will come directly from these peoples' capabilities.'* (Linda Fleet)

But not everyone was so sanguine about the rise of the Design department. *'It is undeniable that relationships between the designers and other parts of the company have been under strain recently. I suppose it is, to some extent, inevitable. After all, they really do need the freedom to design as they wish. I can understand it when they get frustrated at some of the constraints which we have to work under in the manufacturing or distribution parts of the business. They also should be able to expect a professional level of service from us. Yet the truth is that they make most of the problems themselves. They sometimes don't seem to understand the consequences or implications of their design decisions or the promises they make to the design houses. More seriously, they don't really understand that we could actually help them do their job better if they cooperated a bit more. In fact, I now see*

some of our design house partners' designers more than I do our own designers. The Villessi designers are always in my factory and we have developed some really good relationships.' (Grant Williams)

The second major issue concerned sales forecasting, and again there were two different views. Grant Williams was convinced that forecasts should be improved. *'Every Friday morning we devise a schedule of production and distribution for the following week. Yet, usually before Tuesday morning, it has had to be significantly changed because of unexpected orders coming in from our customers' weekend sales. This causes tremendous disruption to both manufacturing and distribution operations. If sales could be forecast more accurately we would achieve far higher utilisation, better customer service and, I believe, significant cost savings.'*

However, Linda Fleet saw things differently. *'Look, I do understand Grant's frustration, but after all, this is a fashion business. By definition it is impossible to forecast accurately. In terms of month-by-month sales volumes we are in fact pretty accurate, but trying to make a forecast for every week end every product is almost impossible to do accurately. Sorry, that's just the nature of the business we're in. In fact, although Grant complains about our lack of forecast accuracy, he always does a great job in responding to unexpected customer demand.'*

Jim Thompson, the Managing Director, summed up his view of the current situation. *'Particularly significant has been our alliances with the Italian and German design houses. In effect we are positioning ourselves as a complete service partner to the designers. We have a world class design capability together with manufacturing, order processing, order taking and distribution services. These abilities allow us to develop genuinely equal partnerships which integrate us into the whole industry's activities.'*

Linda Fleet also saw an increasing role for collaborative arrangements. *'It may be that we are seeing a fundamental change in how we do business within our industry. We have always seen ourselves as primarily a company that satisfies consumer desires through the medium of providing good service to retailers. The new partnership arrangements put us more into the 'business-to-business' sector. I don't have any problem with this in principle, but I'm a little anxious as to how much it gets us into areas of business beyond our core expertise.'*

The final issue which was being debated within the company was longer term, and particularly important. *'The two big changes we have made in this company have both happened because we exploited a strength we already had within the company. Moving into Concept products was only possible because we brought our high-tech precision expertise that we had developed in the* aerospace sector into the homeware sector where none of our new competitors could match our manufacturing excellence. Then, when we moved into design house partnerships we did so because we had a set of designers who could command respect from the world-class design houses with whom we formed partnerships. So what is the next move for us? Do we expand globally? We are strong in Europe but nowhere else in the world. Do we extend our design scope into other markets, such as furniture? If so, that would take us into areas where we have no manufacturing expertise. We are great at plastic injection moulding, but if we tried any other manufacturing processes, we would be no better than, and probably worse than, other firms with more experience. So what's the future for us?' (Jim Thompson, CEO CDS)

QUESTIONS

1 Why is operations management important in CDS?

2 Draw a 'four Vs' profile for the company's products/services.

3 What would you recommend to the company if they asked you to advise them in improving their operations?

**CASE
6**

Case date
2001

New supply chain strategies at old M&S

© Alan Harrison and Jane Pavitt

Introduction

Marks & Spencer (M&S) is a leading retailer of clothing, food, homeware and financial services. Around 10 million customers per week are served in around 300 UK stores. The company was started in 1884, when Michael Marks (a Russian-born Polish refugee) opened a stall at Leeds Kirkgate Market. By 1997, M&S had grown into an international group with an annual sales turnover in excess of £8 billion – combined with one of the highest net margins in retailing.

M&S experienced a wrenching time since those glory days, having become highly vulnerable in its core customer base – women aged between 35 and 55. The very advantages that M&S had painstakingly built up became liabilities in the market downturn of autumn, 1998. For example, lengthy supply chain procedures meant that the company was buying 9 to 12 months ahead of the market. Traditionally M&S bought twice a year for spring and autumn with phased buying in between – that is, there were just two main sales 'seasons' per year. Nimbler competitors exploited many seasons per year for fashion items at one end of the market, and everyday low pricing that M&S could not match at the other. The M&S counter-offensive took a long time to formulate. Luc Vandevelde, the third CEO in as many years, said in his annual review to shareholders in 2001:

'...we have been able to conduct a thorough strategic review. Although some of the decisions we've taken are painful, they are necessary if M&S is to return to growth, and they will improve our ability to compete and respond more quickly to operational demands.'

As part of this strategic review, the UK retail management team, led by Roger Holmes, developed an operational plan that envisaged building on the strengths of M&S and exploiting new growth opportunities. A key part of the recovery plan included major improvements in product appeal, availability and value in order to rebuild relationships with the core womenswear customer base.

A former supplier's view

Many of the 'painful decisions' related to Marks & Spencer's traditional UK supply base, which had been decimated in the scramble to reduce costs. In some ways, this had made the slowness to respond to market changes even worse. A former employee of a former M&S supplier, which has now closed most of its UK factories, commented on the recent changes:

'Three years ago M&S operated a very standard, very formalised route from order to contract, production and distribution. Each item had to have an M&S garment number as identification all the way through production, which precluded suppliers from manufacturing items for other retailers. More recent supplier rationalisation has changed this approach, but it is still very formalised and in reality a more informal approach is taken on a daily basis to actually get things done.'

Much of the manufacture of M&S products had been transferred abroad. There is very little capital expenditure in clothing. Typically, raw materials account for 50 per cent of the product cost, and labour for 30 per cent. Labour costs were much cheaper in countries like China, Cambodia and Bangladesh, but this has had a significant impact on lead-times: it takes four to six weeks to ship from the Far East. Airfreight is used sparingly, as it has not been possible to get the type of costs required for routine airfreight.

When buying standard ranges there is a balance between buying few colour ranges at higher volumes, or more colours at lower volumes. Combinations add to complexity: if there are eight colours and eight sizes, there are 64 stock keeping units (SKUs) in the range. M&S bought in a ratio across sizes based on sales history, but actual sales in a season – especially colours – were difficult to forecast. Responding to changes in volume and mix in the marketplace was difficult enough for the ponderous M&S systems, but the company's insistence on a single brand brought further problems:

'M&S procedures do not allow flexibility for short lead times. Had they agreed to sub-brand in the past, it would have been possible to produce to different quality standards for different product ranges.'

New product development was also slow and costly. All suppliers were asked to develop all ranges – M&S would then decide who would manufacture what and where. This increased development costs all round. The company has become more skilled at assessing supplier capabilities in advance. Suppliers who are low-cost producers receive orders for commodity products, while those with strengths in product or material development receive orders for more innovative lines.

Improving the supply chain

M&S identified opportunities to reduce supply chain costs substantially, and achieved targeted savings of £120 million in 2000. The priorities were to eliminate duplication and to increase transparency. Some of the savings were achieved by using fewer suppliers and by working more effectively with them. This enabled M&S to get goods to the shops faster and to respond more quickly to emerging customer demands. By re-establishing closer working relationships with its supply partners – historically a unique strength – M&S wanted to achieve further improvements in quality, value, product appeal and availability.

Using information about customer preferences, buyers were better able to give suppliers the information needed to be more flexible and efficient in production. The company admitted that the speed of the changes made, and the replacement of a major supplier, did create availability problems in the autumn and spring of 2000/2001 – particularly in knitwear and lingerie. A focus on the 500 best-selling products, particularly basic items like socks and knickers, sought to ensure that customers noticed an improvement in availability.

Improving the segmentation of clothing

M&S has concentrated on regaining the loyalty of its core customers, who prefer classically stylish clothes. In the past, the company had resisted splitting its traditional *St Michael* brand name, preferring to leverage the power of a single name that became synonymous with the company. As part of its new plan to segment products across different lifestyles, the company recognised that this was no longer tenable. For example, George Davies was appointed to design and supply a collection for the fashion-conscious woman. Davies had risen to fame as a result of making the retailer Next well known on the UK high street with his innovative designs and methods, and by his subsequent success in developing the *George* range of clothing at Asda supermarkets. His sub-brand at M&S was labelled *per una*, and 50 selected M&S stores were laid out by lifestyle to give impact and clarity to the display. Supply chain issues were also attended to.

'per una is "ring fenced" within the M&S system so that the range can be produced to a different standard. This enables George Davies to achieve a four-week turnaround.'

Another range called *The Autograph* was created by top designers to offer fashion items at High Street prices. A compromise was reached in sourcing this range, which was originally produced in UK factories but moved to Portugal. This had the benefit of cheaper labour costs than the UK and shorter lead-times than the Far East.

M&S also planned to regain the confidence of its customers in the quality and fit of its clothing. It chose to sharpen pricing by rebalancing the price structure and by extending the range of entry prices. The aim was to deliver 'aspirational quality at great value'.

Womenswear ranges for autumn 2001

M&S further segmented its womenswear products to appeal to different lifestyles by introducing a number of ranges and sub-brands in addition to *per una* and *The Autograph*, including *The Perfect Collection* and *The Classic Collection*.

The Perfect Collection
The Perfect Collection focused on classically stylish merchandise for core customers. There are 60 lines for women and men which 'return to basics', and they include plain, white shirts, black roll-neck sweaters and jeans. With many items machine washable, non-iron and tumble-dry friendly, they're aimed at the customer with a busy lifestyle who is looking for quality and value at a reasonable price. The brochure described them as 'timeless essentials that you can wear with just about anything'.

The Classic Collection
The Classic Collection was aimed at the more mature customer, and the advertising concentrated on design, comfort, long-lasting style and versatility – 'Every piece in

The Classic Collection is designed to skim and flatter the natural body shape, whatever your size'. *The Classic Collection* is a range of smart, elegant clothes, made from high-quality fabrics at value-for-money prices. 'It's a timeless collection that reflects your style and finesse, and not just the latest fashion.'

The Autograph range

The category manager, Liz Alcock, states: 'The *Autograph* philosophy is to bring cutting-edge design to a wider audience within a unique environment'. Like *per una*, *The Autograph* label, which was launched in the spring/summer 2000 range, was made available in selected stores only. M&S recruited some of the best designers in the business – such as Julien Macdonald, Philip Treacy and Sonja Nuttall – to create womenswear, menswear and accessories collections. For example, Philip Treacy's hat collection was launched in 15 M&S *Autograph* boutiques nationwide in March 2001 and comprised 18 hats and 10 bags with no more than 60 of each colourway and style. *Autograph* brings top designer collections to M&S customers at high street prices, within a designer boutique environment.

per una

This high-quality range was designed to appeal to a broad catchment at competitive prices, and was launched in September 2001 into selected stores. The target customers were fashion-conscious women aged between 25 and 35, sizes 8–18. The aim was to provide 'superb designs at very affordable prices'. George Davies controls the supply chain, including sourcing and merchandising as well as control of the look of the selling space in store. In the brochure, he says *per una* embodies principles of 'the highest quality materials … designs inspired by the very latest trends … limited editions … individual cuts for every size … fanatical attention to detail … ease of shopping'. The 300-piece collection was sourced from 90 suppliers from Hong Kong to central Europe. Production runs were short with no repeats, and speed of reaction was important to ensure that goods made it from design concept to shop rails in weeks not months.

In *Marks & Spencer Magazine*, September 2001, George Davies was quoted as saying:

'I know women don't want to see loads of the same thing around. It's OK for plainer pieces, but if it's distinctive, they want it to be rare. Which is why we'll have a series of limited-edition items introduced throughout the life of a three-month collection – so buy them because they won't be in store for long.'

Unlike other ranges in store where up to 20 of a style can be seen together, *per una* items were presented in small numbers, making each style 'special' and more exclusive. *per una* was 10 per cent more expensive than the M&S main range. However, the rollout programme had to be scaled down because the company could not keep up with higher than expected customer demand.

Customer comments

Two M&S customers were asked: 'What are you looking for?' and 'What is important to you when considering buying a standard item or a high fashion item?' The first was a smartly dressed lady, aged 54, who said:

'For a standard item it's important that my size is available but quality and price are also important. In terms of quality, a jumper, for example, must be value for money, wash well and not require specialist washing (hand wash or dry clean!). For a premium item I don't want to be wearing something that is instantly recognisable as M&S – if I'm paying a premium price, therefore, "exclusive" design is a must. Quality is also important if I'm paying a higher price, as it must be well made and expected to last.'

The second customer, a fashionably dressed lady, aged 33, was asked the same questions, and said:

'I get very frustrated if an item is not available in my size. I am annoyed when I find that it is only currently in stock in sizes 8–10 as the larger sizes have sold out. They never seem to have enough of the bigger sizes. For a standard item I expect value for money and a "reasonable" quality – colour not to fade and it won't shrink when washed. Availability of a variety of colour shades for a shirt or jumper is helpful but not a key driver (size availability is key). For premium/high-fashion items, quality is not as important to me as design. If it's a high-fashion item I expect to wear it only a few times before replacing it. I would not make a specific trip to a store to buy such an item from M&S (unlike a standard item). It would tend to be more of an impulse purchase.'

Questions

1 *What market segments do the three different product ranges serve? Assume that the* Perfect *and* Classic *ranges serve essentially the same segment.*

2 *What are the order winners and qualifiers for these different ranges?*

3 *What are the different logistics performance objectives for the different product groups? Fill in the following table:*

	Perfect and *Classic* ranges	*Autograph* range	*per una* range
Product range			
Design changes			
Price			
Quality			
Sales volumes SKU			
Order winners			
Order qualifiers			
Operations priorities			

The M&S website is at: *www.marksandspencer.com*

Case study
Long Ridge Gliding Club[10]

Long Ridge Gliding Club is a not-for-profit organization run by its members. The large grass airfield is located on the crest of a ridge about 400 metres above sea level. It is an ideal place to practise ridge soaring and cross-country flying. The gliders are launched using a winch machine which can propel them from a standing start to around 110 kilometres per hour (70 mph), 300 metres above the airfield, in just five seconds. The club is housed in a set of old farm buildings with simple but comfortable facilities for members. A bar and basic catering services are provided by the club steward and inexpensive bunk-rooms are available for club members wishing to stay overnight.

The club has a current membership of nearly 150 pilots who range in ability from novice to expert. While some members have their own gliders, the club has a fleet of three single-seater and three twin-seater gliders available to its members. The club also offers trial flights to members of the public. (In order to provide insurance cover they actually sell a three-month membership with a 'free' flight at the start.) These 'casual flyers' can book flights in advance or just turn up and fly on a first-come, first-served basis. The club sells trial-flight gift vouchers which are popular as birthday and Christmas presents. The club's brochure and web site encourage people to:

'Experience the friendly atmosphere and excellent facilities and enjoy the thrill of soaring above Long Ridge's dramatic scenery. For just £70 you could soon be in the air. Phone now or just turn up and our knowledgeable staff will be happy to advise you. We have a team of professional instructors dedicated to make this a really memorable experience.'

The average flight for a trial lesson is around 10 minutes. If the conditions are right the customer may be lucky and get a longer flight although at busy times the instructors may feel under pressure to return to the ground to give another lesson. Sometimes when the weather is poor, low cloud and wind in the wrong direction, almost not fit for flying at all, the instructors still do their best to get people airborne but they are restricted to a 'circuit': a takeoff, immediate circle and land. This only takes two minutes. Circuits are also used to help novice pilots practise landings and takeoffs. At the other end of the scale many of the club's experienced pilots can travel long distances and fly back to the airfield. The club's record for the longest flight is 755 kilometres, taking off from the club's airfield and landing back on the same airfield eight hours later, never having touched the ground. (They take sandwiches and drinks and a bottle they can use to relieve themselves!)

The club has three part-time employees: a club steward, an office administrator and a mechanic. In the summer months the club also employs a winch driver (for launching the gliders) and two qualified flying instructors. Throughout the whole year essential tasks such as maintaining the gliders, getting them out of the hangar and towing them to the launch point, staffing the winches, keeping the flying log, bringing back gliders, and providing look-out cover is undertaken on a voluntary basis by club members. It takes a minimum of five experienced people (club members) to be able to launch one glider. The club's membership includes ten qualified instructors who, together with the two paid summer instructors, provide instruction in two-seater gliders for the club's members and the casual flyers.

When club members come to fly they are expected to arrive by 9.30 am and be prepared to stay all day to help each other and any casual flyers get airborne while they wait their turn to fly. On a typical summer's day there might be ten club members requiring instruction plus four casual flyers and also six members with their own gliders who have to queue up with the others for a launch hoping for a single long-distance flight. In the winter months there would typically be six members, one casual flyer and six experienced pilots. Club members would hope to have three flights on a good day, with durations of between two and forty (average ten) minutes per flight depending on conditions. However, if the weather conditions change they may not get a flight. Last year there were 180 days when flying took place, 140 in the 'summer' season and 40 in the 'winter'. Club members are charged an £8.00 winch fee each time they take to the air. In addition, if they are using one of the club's gliders, they are charged 50p per minute that they are in the air.

Bookings for trial flights and general administration are dealt with by the club's administrator who is based in a cabin close to the car park and works most weekday mornings from 9.00 am to 1.00 pm. An answerphone takes messages at other times. The launch point is out of sight and 1.5 km from the cabin but a safe walking route is signposted. Club members can let themselves onto the airfield and drive to the launch point. At the launch point the casual flyers might have to stand and wait for some time until a club member has time to find out what they want. Even when a flight has been pre-booked casual flyers may then be kept waiting, on the exposed and often windy airfield, for up to two hours before their flight, depending on how many club members are present. Occasionally they will turn up for a pre-booked trial flight and will be turned away because either the weather is unsuitable or there are not enough club members to get a glider into the air. The casual flyers are encouraged to help out with the routine tasks but often seem reluctant to do so. After their flight they are left to find their own way back to their cars.

Income from the casual flyers is seen to be small compared to membership income and launch fees but the club's management committee views casual flying as a 'loss leader' to generate club memberships which are £350 per annum. The club used to generate a regular surplus of around £10,000 per year which is used to upgrade the gliders and other facilities. However, insurance costs have risen dramatically due to their crashing and severely damaging four gliders during the last two years. Two of the accidents resulted in the deaths of one member and one casual flyer and serious injuries to three other members.

The club's committee is under some pressure from members to end trial flights because they reduce the number of flights members can have in a day. Some members have complained that they sometimes spend most of their day working to get casual flyers into the air and miss out on flying themselves. Although they provide a useful source of income for the hard-pressed club (around 700 were sold in the previous year), only a handful have been converted into club memberships.

Questions

1 Evaluate the service to club members and casual flyers by completing a table similar to Table 3.1.

2 Chart the five performance objectives to show the differing expectations of club members and casual flyers and compare these with the actual service delivered.

3 What advice would you give to the chairman?

Case study
Boys and Boden (B&B)

*'There **must** be a better way of running this place!'*, said Dean Hammond, recently recruited General Manager of B&B, as he finished a somewhat stressful conversation with a complaining customer, a large and loyal local building contractor. *'We had six weeks to make their special staircase, and we are still late. I'll have to persuade one of the joiners to work overtime this weekend to get everything ready for Monday. We never seem to get complaints about quality . . . our men always do an excellent job, but there is usually a big backlog of work, so how can we set priorities? We could do the most profitable work first, or the work for our biggest customers, or the jobs which are most behind. In practice, we try to satisfy everyone as best we can, but inevitably someone's order will be late. On paper, each job should be quite profitable, since we build in a big allowance for waste, and for timber defects. And we know the work content of almost any task we would have to do, and this is the basis of our estimating system. But, overall, the department isn't very profitable in comparison to our other operations, and most problems seem to end up with higher-than-anticipated costs and late deliveries!'*

Boys and Boden was a small, successful, privately owned timber and building materials merchant based in a small town. Over the years it had established its large Joinery Department, which made doors, windows, staircases and other timber products, all to the exact special requirements of the customers, comprising numerous local and regional builders. In addition, the joiners would cut and prepare special orders of timber, such as non-standard sections, and special profiles including old designs of skirting board, sometimes at very short notice while the customers waited. Typically, for joinery items, the customer provided simple dimensioned sketches of the required products. These were then passed to the central Estimating/Quotations Department which, in conjunction with the Joinery Manager, calculated costs and prepared a written quotation which was faxed to the customer. This first stage was normally completed within two or three days, but on occasions could take a week or more. On receipt of an order, the original sketches and estimating details were passed back to the Joinery Manager across the yard, who roughly scheduled them into his plan, allocating them to individual craftsmen as they became available. Most of the joiners were capable of making any product, and enjoyed the wide variety of challenging work.

The Joinery Department appeared congested and somewhat untidy, but everyone believed that this was acceptable and normal for job shops, since there was no single flow route for materials. Whatever the design of the item being made, or the quantity, it was normal for the

joiner to select the required timber from the storage building across the yard. The timber was then prepared using a planer/thicknesser. After that, the joiner would use a variety of processes, depending on the product. The timber could be machined into different cross-sectional shapes, cut into component lengths using a radial arm saw, joints formed by hand tools, or using a mortise/tenon machine, and so on. Finally the products would be glued and assembled, sanded smooth by hand or machine, and treated with preservatives, stains or varnishes if required. All the large and more expensive machines were grouped together by type (for example, saws) or were single pieces of equipment shared by all 10 or so joiners.

Dean described what one might observe on a random visit to the Joinery Department: *'One or two long staircases partly assembled, and crossing several work areas; large door frames on trestles being assembled; stacks of window components for a large contract being prepared and jointed, and so on. Off-cuts and wood shavings are scattered around the work area, but are cleared periodically when they get in the way or form a hazard. The joiners try to fit in with each other over the use of machinery, so are often working on several, part-finished items at once. Varnishing or staining* has to be done when it's quiet – for example, evenings or weekends – or outside, to avoid dust contamination. Long off-cuts are stacked around the workshop, to be used up on any future occasion when these lengths or sections are required. However, it is often easier to take a new length of timber for each job, so the off-cuts do tend to build up over time. Unfortunately, everything I have described is getting worse as we get busier . . . our sales are increasing so the system is getting more congested. The joiners are almost climbing over each other to do their work. Unfortunately, despite having more orders, the department has remained stubbornly unprofitable!

Whilst analysing in detail the lack of profit, we were horrified to find that, for the majority of orders, the actual times booked by the joiners exceeded the estimated times by up to 50 per cent. Sometimes this was attributable to new, inexperienced joiners. Although fully trained and qualified, they might lack the experience needed to complete a complex job in the time an estimator would expect, but there had been no feedback of this to the individual. We put one of these men on doors only; having overcome his initial reluctance, he has become our enthusiastic "door expert", and gets closely involved in quotations too, so he always does his work within the time estimates! However, the main time losses were found to be the result of general delays caused by congestion, interference, double handling and rework to rectify in-process damage. Moreover, we found that a joiner walked an average of nearly 5 km a day, usually carrying around bits of wood.

When I did my operations management course on my MBA, the professor described the application of cellular manufacturing and JIT. From what I can remember, the idea seemed to be to get better flow, reducing the times and distances in the process, and thus achieving quicker through-put times. That is just what we need, but these concepts were explained in the context of high-volume, repetitive production of bicycles, whereas everything we make is "one-offs". However, although we do make a lot of different staircases, they all use roughly the same process steps:

1 Cutting timber to width and length
2 Sanding
3 Machining
4 Tenoning
5 Manual assembly (glue and wedges).

We have a lot of unused factory floor-space, so it would be relatively easy to set up a self-contained staircase cell. There is huge demand for special stairs in this region, but also a lot of competing small joinery businesses which can beat us on price and lead time. So we go to a lot of trouble quoting for stairs, but only win about 20 per cent of the business. If we got the cell idea to work, we could be more competitive on price and delivery, hence winning more orders. I know we will need a lot more volume to justify establishing the cell, so it's really a case of "chicken and egg"!'

Questions

1 To what extent could (or should) Dean expect to apply the philosophies and techniques of JIT described in this chapter to the running of a staircase cell?

2 What are likely to be the main categories of costs and benefits in establishing the cell? Are there any non-financial benefits which should be taken into account?

3 At what stage, and how, should Dean sell his idea to the Joinery Manager and the workers?

4 How different would the cell work be to that in the main Joinery Department?

5 Should Dean differentiate the working environment by providing distinctive work-wear such as T-shirts and distinctively painted machines, in order to reinforce a cultural change?

6 What risks are associated with Dean's proposal?

Blackberry Hill Farm

'Six years ago I had never heard of agri-tourism. As far as I was concerned, I had inherited the farm and I would be a farmer all my life.' (Jim Walker, Blackberry Hill Farm)

The 'agri-tourism' that Jim is referring to is 'a commercial enterprise at a working farm, or other agricultural centre, conducted for the enjoyment of visitors that generates supplemental income for the owner'. 'Farming has become a tough business,' says Jim. 'Low world prices, a reduction in subsidies, and increasingly uncertain weather patterns have made it a far more risky business than when I first inherited the farm. Yet, because of our move into the tourist trade we are flourishing. Also . . . I've never had so much fun in my life'. But, Jim warns, agri-tourism isn't for everyone. 'You have to think carefully. Do you really want to do it? What kind of life style do you want? How open-minded are you to new ideas? How business-minded are you? Are you willing to put a lot of effort into marketing your business? Above all, do you like working with people? If you had rather be around cows than people, it isn't the business for you.'

History

Blackberry Hill Farm was a 200-hectare mixed farm in the south of England when Jim and Mandy Walker inherited it 15 years ago. It was primarily a cereal growing operation with a small dairy herd, some fruit and vegetable growing and mixed woodland that was protected by local preservation laws. Six years ago it had become evident to Jim and Mandy that they may have to rethink how the farm was being managed. 'We first started a pick-your-own (PYO) operation because our farm is close to

Source: Fancy/Veer/Corbis

several large centres of population. Also the quantities of fruit and vegetables that we were producing were not large enough to interest the commercial buyers. Entering the PYO market was a reasonable success and in spite of making some early mistakes, it turned our fruit and vegetable growing operation from making a small loss to making a small profit. Most importantly, it gave us some experience of how to deal with customers face-to-face and of how to cope with unpredictable demand. The biggest variable in PYO sales is weather. Most business occurs at the weekends between late spring and early autumn. If rain keeps customers away during part of those weekends, nearly all sales have to occur in just a few days.'

Within a year of opening up the PYO operation Jim and Mandy had decided to reduce the area devoted to cereals and increase their fruit and vegetable growing capability. At the same time they organised a Petting Zoo that allowed children to mix with, feed and touch various animals.

'We already had our own cattle and poultry but we extended the area and brought in pigs and goats. Later we also introduced some rabbits, ponies and donkeys, and even a small bee keeping operation.' At the same time the farm started building up its collection of 'farm heritage' exhibits. These were static displays of old farm implements and 'recreations' of farming processes together with information displays. This had always been a personal interest of Jim's and it allowed him to convert two existing farm outbuilding to create a 'Museum of Farming Heritage'.

The year after, they introduced tractor rides for visitors around the whole farm and extended the petting zoo and farming tradition exhibits further. But the most significant investment was in the 'Preserving Kitchen'. 'We had been looking for some way of using the surplus fruits and vegetable that we occasionally accumulated and also for some kind of products that we could sell in a farm shop. We started the Preserving Kitchen to make jams and fruit, vegetables and sauces preserved in jars. The venture was an immediate success. We started making just 50 kilograms of preserves a week, within three months that had grown 300 kilogrammes a week and we are now producing around 1,000 kilogrammes a week, all under the 'Blackberry Hill Farm' label.' The following year the preserving kitchen was extended and

Table 8.2(a) Number of visitors last year

Month	Total visitors	Month	Total visitors
January	1,006	August	15,023
February	971	September	12,938
March	2,874	October	6,687
April	6,622	November	2,505
May	8,905	December	3,777
June	12,304	**Total**	**88,096**
July	14,484	Average	7,341.33

Table 8.2(b) Farm opening times*

January to Mid-March	Wednesday–Sunday	10.00–16.00
Mid-March to May	Tuesday–Sunday	9.00–18.00
May to September	All week	8.30–19.00
October to November	Tuesday–Sunday	10.00–16.00
December	Tuesday–Sunday	9.00–18.00

*Special evening events at Easter, summer weekends and Christmas.

a viewing area added. 'It was a great attraction from the beginning,' says Mandy. 'We employed ladies from the local village to make the preserves. They are all extrovert characters, so when we asked them to dress up in traditional 'farmers wives' type clothing they were happy to do it. The visitors love it, especially the good natured repartee with our ladies. The ladies also enjoy giving informal history lessons when we get school parties visiting us.'

Within the last two years, the farm has further extended its preserving kitchen, farm shop, exhibits and petting zoo. It has also introduced a small adventure playground for the children, a café serving drinks and its own produce, a picnic area and a small bakery. The bakery was also open to view by customers and staffed by bakers in traditional dress. 'It's a nice little visitor attraction,' says Mandy, 'and it gives us another opportunity to squeeze more value out of our own products.' Table 8.2(a) shows last year's visitor numbers; Table 8.2(b) shows the farm's opening times.

Demand

The number of visitors to the farm was extremely seasonal. From a low point in January and February, when most people just visited the farm shop, the spring and summer months could be very busy, especially on public holidays. The previous year Mandy had tracked the number of visitors arriving at the farm each day. 'It is easy to record the number of people visiting the farm attractions, because they pay the entrance charge. What we had not done before is include the people who just visited the farm shop and bakery that can be accessed both from within the farm and from the car park. We estimate that the number of people visiting the shop but not the farm ranges from 74 per cent in February down to around 15 per cent in August.' Figure 8.13 shows the number of visitors in the previous year's August. 'What

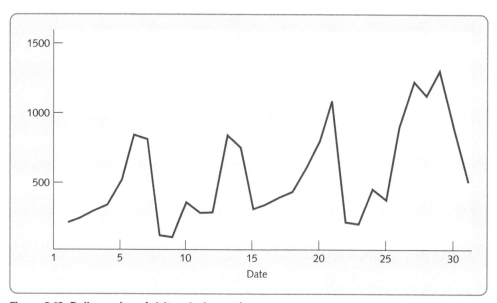

Figure 8.13 Daily number of visitors in August last year

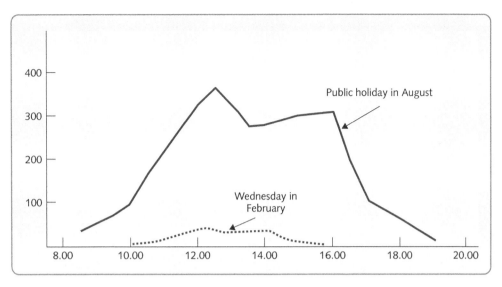

Figure 8.14 Visitor arrivals, public holiday in August and a Wednesday in February

our figures do not include are those people who visit the shop but don't buy anything. This is unlikely to be a large number.'

Mandy had also estimated the average stay at the farm and/or farm shop. She reckoned that in winter time the average stay was 45 minutes, but in August in climbed to 3.1 hours.

Current issues

Both Jim and Mandy agreed that their lives had fundamentally changed over the last few years. Income from visitors and from the Blackberry Hill brand of preserves now accounted for 70 per cent of the farm's revenue. More importantly, the whole enterprise was significantly more profitable than it had ever been. Nevertheless, the farm faced a number of issues.

The first was the balance between its different activities. Jim was particularly concerned that the business remained a genuine farm. *'When you look at the revenue per hectare, visitor and production activities bring in far more revenue than conventional agricultural activities. However, if we push the agri-tourism too far we become no better than a theme park. We represent something more than this to our visitors. They come to us partly because of what we represent as well as what we actually do. I am not sure that we would want to grow much more. Anyway, more visitors would mean that we have to extend the car park. That would be expensive, and although it would be necessary, it does not directly bring in any more revenue. There are already parking problems during peak period and we have had complaints from the police that our visitors park inappropriately on local roads.'*

'There is also the problem of complexity. Every time we introduce a new attraction, the whole business gets that little bit more complex to manage. Although we enjoy it tremendously, both Mandy and I are spreading ourselves thinly over an ever widening range of activities.' Mandy was also concerned over this. *'I'm starting to feel that my time is being taken up in managing the day-to-day problems of the business. This does not leave time either for thinking about the overall direction in which we should be going, or spending time talking with the staff. That is why we both see this coming year as a time for consolidation and for smoothing out the day-to-day problems of managing the business, particularly the queuing, which is getting excessive at busy times. That is why this year we are limiting ourselves to just one new venture for the business.'*

Staff management was also a concern for Mandy. The business had grown to over 80 (almost all part-time and seasonal) employees. *'We have become a significant employer in the area. Most of our employees are still local people working part-time for extra income but we are also now employing 20 students during the summer period and, last year, eight agricultural students from Eastern Europe. But now, labour is short in this part of the country and it is becoming more difficult to attract local people, especially to produce Blackberry Hill Farm Preserves. Half of the Preserving Kitchen staff work all year, with the other employed during the summer and autumn periods. But most of them would prefer guaranteed employment throughout the year.'*

Table 8.3 gives more details of some of the issues of managing the facilities at the farm, and Table 8.4 shows the demand and production of preserves month by month through the previous year.

Table 8.3 The farm's main facilities and some of the issues concerned with managing them

Facility	Issues
Car park	• 85 car parking spaces, 4 × 40-seater tour bus spaces.
Fixed exhibits, etc. Recreation of old farmhouse kitchen, recreation of barnyard, old-fashioned milking parlour, various small exhibits on farming past and present, adventure playground, ice cream and snack stands.	• Most exhibits in, or adjacent to, the farm museum. • At peak times helpers are dressed in period costume to entertain visitors. • Feedback indicates customers find exhibits more interesting than they thought they would. • Visitors free to look when they wish absorbs demand from busy facilities.
Tractor rides One tractor towing decorated covered cart with maximum capacity of 30 people. Tour takes around 20 minutes on average (including stops). Waits ten minutes between tours except at peak times when tractor circulates continuously.	• Tractor acts both as transport and entertainment. Approximately 60 per cent of visitors stay on for the whole tour; 40 per cent use it as 'hop-on hop-off' facility. • Overloaded at peak times, long queues building. • Feedback indicates it is popular, except for queuing. • Jim reluctant to invest in further cart and tractor.
Pick-your-own area Largest single facility on the farm. Use local press, dedicated telephone line (answering machine) and website to communicate availability of fruit and vegetables. Check-out and weighing area next to farm shop, also displays picked produce and preserves etc. for sale.	• Very seasonal and weather dependent, both for supply and demand. • Farm plans for a surplus over visitor demand: uses surplus in preserves. • Six weighing/paying stations at undercover checkout area. Queues develop at peak times. Feedback indicates some dissatisfaction with this. • Can move staff from farm shop to help with checkout in busy periods, but farm shop also tends to be busy at the same time. • Considering using packers at pay stations to speed up the process.
Petting Zoo Accommodation for smaller animals, including sheep and pigs. Large animals (cattle, horses) brought to viewing area daily. Visitors can view all animals and handle/stroke most animals under supervision.	• Approximately 50 per cent of visitors view Petting Zoo. • Number of staff in attendance varies between 0 (off-peak) and 5 (peak periods). • The area can get congested during peak periods. • Staff need to be skilled at managing children.
Preserving Kitchen Boiling vats, mixing vats, jar sterilising equipment, etc. Visitor viewing area can hold 15 people comfortably. Average length of stay 7 minutes in off-season, 14 minutes in peak season.	• Capacity of kitchen is theoretically 4,500 kilogrammes per month on a five-day week and 6,000 kilogrammes on a seven-day week. • In practice, capacity varies with season because of interaction with visitors. Can be as low as 5,000 kg on a seven-day week in summer, or up to 5,000 kg on a five-day week in winter. • Shelf life of products is on average 12 months. • Current storage area can hold 16,000 kilogrammes.
Bakery Contains mixing and shaping equipment, commercial oven, cooling racks, display stand, etc. Just installed doughnut-making machine. All pastries contain farm's preserved fruit.	• Starting to become a bottleneck since doughnut-making machine installed; visitors like watching it. • Products also on sale at farm shop adjacent to bakery. • Would be difficult to expand this area because of building constraints.
Farm shop and café Started by selling farm's own products exclusively. Now sells a range of products from farms in the region and wider. Started selling frozen menu dishes (lasagne, goulash, etc.) produced off-peak in the preserving kitchen.	• The most profitable part of the whole enterprise, Jim and Mandy would like to extend the retailing and café operation. • Shop includes area for cooking displays, cake decoration, fruit dipping (in chocolate), etc. • Some congestion in shop at peak times but little visitor dissatisfaction. • More significant queuing for café in peak periods. • Considering allowing customers to place orders before they tour the farm's facilities and collect their purchases later. • Retailing more profitable per square metre than café.

Table 8.4 Preserve demand and production (previous year)

Month	Demand (kg)	Cumulative demand (kg)	Production (kg)	Cumulative product (kg)	Inventory (kg)
January	682	682	4,900	4,900	4,218
February	794	1,476	4,620	9,520	8,044
March	1,106	2,582	4,870	14,390	11,808
April	3,444	6.026	5,590	19,980	13,954
May	4,560	10,586	5,840	25,820	15,234
June	6,014	16,600	5,730	31,550	14,950
July	9,870	26,470	5,710	37,260	10,790
August	13,616	40,086	5,910	43,170	3,084
September	5,040	45,126	5,730	48,900	3,774
October	1,993	47,119	1,570*	50,470	3,351
November	2,652	49,771	2,770*	53,240	3,467
December	6,148	55,919	4,560	57,800	1,881
Average demand	4,660			Average inventory	7,880

*Technical problems reduced production level.

Where next?

By the 'consolidation' and improvement of 'day-to-day' activities, Jim and Mandy mean that they wanted to increase their revenue, while at the same time reducing the occasional queues that they knew could irritate their visitors, preferably without any significant investment in extra capacity. They are also concerned to be able to offer more stable employment to the Preserving Kitchen 'ladies' throughout the year, who would produce at a near constant rate. However, they were not sure if this could be done without storing the products for so long that their shelf life would be seriously affected. There was no problem with the supply of produce to keep production level, less than 2 per cent of the fruit and vegetables that go into their preserves are actually grown on the farm. The remainder were bought at wholesale markets, although this was not generally understood by customers.

Of the many ideas being discussed as candidates for the 'one new venture' for next year, two are emerging as particularly attractive. Jim likes the idea of developing a Maize Maze, a type of attraction that had become increasingly popular in Europe and North America in the last five years. It involves planting a field of maize (corn) and, once grown, cutting through a complex serious of paths in the form of a maze. Evidence from other farms indicate that a maze would be extremely attractive to visitors and Jim reckons that it could account for up to an extra 10,000 visitors during the summer period.

Designed as a separate activity with its own admission charge, it would require an investment of around £20,000, but generate more than twice that in admission charges as well as attracting more visitors to the farm itself.

Mandy favours the alterative idea – that of building up their business in organised school visits. 'Last year we joined the National Association of Farms for Schools. Their advice is that we could easily become one of the top school attractions in this part of England. Educating visitors about farming tradition is already a major part of what we do. And many of our staff have developed the skills to communicate to children exactly what farm life used to be like. We would need to convert and extend one of our existing underused farm outbuildings to make a 'school room' and that would cost between and £30,000 and £35,000. And although we would need to discount our admission charge substantially, I think we could break even on the investment within around two years.'

QUESTIONS

1 How could the farm's day-to-day operations be improved?

2 What advice would you give Jim and Mandy regarding this year's 'new venture'?

CASE 23

I'll Phone You Back!

Case date
2002   Stuart Chambers

Dave McDonald, owner of Oilpartz Ltd, took off his jacket and sat down at his desk. It was the early morning of his first day back at work after the two-week annual holiday shutdown, and the beginning of Week 1 of the company's financial year. Dave had been pleased that his production team had managed to complete and despatch all existing orders before their holiday. However, this meant that the only new work for them would be any that had come in while they had been away. Dave had about 30 regular customers who valued the exceptional quality and reliability of Oilpartz' workmanship, and its almost unique capabilities for producing small quantities of very complex, special components.

Oilpartz specialised in producing some of the larger pipeline components used on rigs, production platforms and on-shore facilities of the oil industry. There were also a few customers in the chemicals and heavy engineering industries. Because of the size and complexity of the parts, machining times were long, and could be up to five hours per component, per operation. As these were mostly used for major capital projects and for planned maintenance, customers usually were happy to accept Oilpartz's normal quoted lead-time of six weeks. Sometimes, however, a regular customer might ask for a quicker delivery, perhaps because of a late design approval or because of an ordering error. Dave always liked to help, but tried to ensure that other customers never suffered as a result of doing such a favour. Also, for the same reason, he never accepted orders for repetitive, high-volume work. Customers usually arranged for all their special raw materials requirements (such as tubes, forgings and rings) to be delivered to the company shortly after placing their orders, a system known as 'free issue'.

By 7.30 a.m., Dave had checked through the new orders received, and was just starting to prepare the schedules, ready for the start of production in half an hour, when the telephone rang. It was Mike Rowlands of Nitro Chemicals, one of Oilpartz' larger and very profitable accounts.

'Dave, it's Mike ... Sorry to bother you so early, but I've a big problem down here that I hope you can help me with! As you know, our main plant has just been shut down for its annual overhaul, and already we've run short of those stainless steel sealing rings – the smaller diameter ones. One of the contract welders used the wrong process settings when fitting them, and we've had to scrap most of his work and start again. You must remember the part – you did some of them for us just a month ago, they're your reference NC11! We really need 20 of them ... well, like yesterday! What could you do to help us out? We only have less than two weeks before the whole plant must be back on stream. If you could start straightaway, we could send the material down to you immediately. I would really be extremely grateful if you could help – and if you need to work overtime, I would be only too willing to pay the extra costs. I just need to know when you could get them ready for us to collect. As you can imagine, this is really critical to us!'

Dave stretched back in his chair and paused a moment before responding:

'I've just got back from holiday, Mike, so I haven't finished the schedule yet. I will see if I can fit in your order, but it sounds a really difficult request. From what I remember, your job took us at least *six* weeks last time, and that was at a relatively quiet time for us. Today we've got quite a full order book after our shutdown. However, we still have the drawings and machining times from before, so I will work out what we can do for you. I understand the urgency, so please give me half an hour or so, and I'll call you back, Mike!'

Dave looked at the list of four jobs that he had just entered in the order book, all of which were for familiar work of a type that was ordered fairly regularly. He then pulled out the corresponding job record cards from the filing cabinet, which gave machining times per operation, per component. Because of the small batch quantities, all operations were undertaken by highly skilled machinists, and any set-up time for each operation was insignificant compared to the long machining times involved. During the machining, each employee normally operated only one machine at a time, so that full attention was given to the quality of each component. This was critical because of the high cost of materials involved, and the high value-added at each stage.

Dave's four highly skilled machinists worked eight hours a day, Monday to Friday. They were usually willing to work some evenings and occasionally at weekends, but Dave had agreed that no one would normally be asked to do more than

Table 23.1 Analysis of orders – in sequence of order placement date

Customer	Part ref.	No. reqd.	Operation route (sequence) and hours per component				Delivery end of week No.
			Op 1	Op 2	Op 3	Op 4	
Alpha Oil	AO6	10	Turn 5	Mill 3	Drill 4	Grind 2.5	4
British Pipelines	BP23	5	Turn 10	Mill 5	Drill 2	Turn 4	3*
Gamma Gases	GG7	10	Mill 2	Drill 3			5
Delta Engineering	DE31	5	Turn 3	Mill 4	Grind 4		6
Nitro Chemicals	NC11	20	Turn 1	Mill 0.5	Drill 1.5	Grind 1.5	urgent

*British Pipelines' order had been sent at the end of the first week of the holiday, and it had requested delivery within five weeks. This customer is Oilpartz's largest and oldest account.

10 hours of overtime. Experience had shown that beyond those hours too many expensive mistakes were being made. Each machinist was multi-skilled and could operate any of the machines. Oilpartz owned two lathes (used for turning, or cutting cylindrical surfaces), one milling machine (used to cut flat areas and slots), one drill (for cutting holes) and a grinding machine (for extremely precise cutting and smooth finishing of surfaces).

Dave summarised the details of all the orders, including the urgent one from Nitro Chemicals, on his office whiteboard. His next tasks would be to turn that into a schedule, and then to phone Mike. He then added the processing times for the current orders and for the Nitro Chemicals enquiry. A copy of this completed information is shown as Table 23.1.

Questions

To answer these questions you should first prepare a blank Gantt chart for scheduling the five machines.

1 *What is the best delivery date (week number and day) that Dave could quote to Mike? Will this affect delivery to the other customers and, therefore, should it be taken on?*

2 *If Dave decided not to give priority to Mike's order, he would then be able to schedule the other four orders in several different ways. Compare and contrast the schedules for:*

- *First come, first served (FCFS)*
- *Due date (DD)*
- *Longest operation time first (LOT)*

In preparing the LOT schedule, you will have to decide whether to consider the operation time for each order at each machine, or overall for all operations. State which assumptions you have made, explaining what you have done, and why.

This case was developed from an unpublished Hancock's Half Hour case with the kind permission of Roy Staughton.

Case study
Trans-European Plastics

Trans-European Plastics (TEP) is one of Europe's largest manufacturers of plastic household items. Its French factory makes a range of over 500 products that are sold to wholesalers and large retailers throughout Europe. The company dispatches orders within 24 hours of receipt using an international carrier. All customers would expect to receive their requirements in full within one week. The manufacturing operation is based on batch production, employing 24 large injection-moulding machines. Weekly production schedules are prepared by the Planning and Control office, detailing the sequence of products (moulds and colours) to be used, the quantity required for each batch, and the anticipated timing of each production run. Mould changes ('set-ups') take on average three hours, at an estimated cost of €500 per set-up.

Concerned about the declining delivery reliability, increased levels of finished goods inventory and falling productivity (apparently resulting from 'split batches' where only part of a planned production batch is produced to overcome immediate shortages), the CEO, Francis Lamouche, employed consultants to undertake a complete review of operations. On 2 January, a full physical inventory check was taken. A representative sample of 20 products from the range is shown in Table 12.7.

Because of current high demand for many products, the backlog of work for planned stock replenishment

Source: Alamy/ArchivBerlin Fotoagentur GmbH

currently averages two weeks, and so all factory orders must be planned at least that far in advance. The re-order quantities (see Table 12.7) had always been established by the Estimating Department at the time when each new product was designed and the manufacturing costs were established, based on Marketing's estimates of likely demand. Recently, however, to minimize the total cost of set-ups and to maximize capacity utilization, all products are planned for a *minimum* production run of 20 hours. The individual re-order levels have not been reviewed for several years, but were originally based on two weeks' average sales at that time. About 20 per cent of the →

Table 12.7 Details of a representative sample of 20 TEP products

Product reference number*	Description	Unit manuf'g variable cost (Euro)	Last 12 mths' sales (000s)	Physical inventory 2 Jan (000s)	Re-order quantity (000s)	Standard moulding rate** (items/hour))
016GH	Storage bin large	2.40	10	0	5	240
033KN	Storage jar + lid	3.60	60	6	4	200
041GH	10 litre bucket	0.75	2,200	360	600	300
062GD	Grecian-style pot	4.50	40	15	20	180
080BR	Bathroom mirror	7.50	5	6	5	250
101KN	1 litre jug	0.90	100	22	20	600
126KN	Pack (10) bag clips	0.45	200	80	50	2,000
143BB	Baby bath	3.75	50	1	2	90
169BB	Baby potty	2.25	60	0	4	180
188BQ	Barbecue table	16.20	10	8	5	120
232GD	Garden bird bath	3.00	2	6	4	200
261GH	Broom head	1.20	60	22	20	400
288KN	Pack (10) clothes pegs	1.50	10	17	50	1,000
302BQ	Barbecue salad fork	0.30	5	12	8	400
351GH	Storage bin small	1.50	25	1	6	300
382KN	Round mixing bowl	0.75	800	25	80	650
421KN	Pasta jar	3.00	1	3	5	220
444GH	Wall hook	0.75	200	86	60	3,000
472GH	Dustbin + lid	9.00	300	3	10	180
506BR	Soap holder	1.20	10	9	20	400

*The reference number uses the following codes for ranges:

BB = Babycare   BQ = Barbecue   BR = Bathroom   GD = Garden   GH = General household   KN = Kitchen

**Moulding rate is for the product as described (e.g. includes lids, or pack quantities).

products are very seasonal (e.g. Garden Range), with peak demand from April to August. Storage bins sell particularly well from October to December.

The European Marketing Manager summarized the current position, *'Our coverage of the market has never been so comprehensive; we are able to offer a full range of household plastics, which appeals to most European tastes. But we will not retain our newly developed markets unless we can give distributors confidence that we will supply all their orders within one week. Unfortunately, at the moment, many receive several deliveries for each order, spread over many weeks. This certainly increases their administrative and handling costs, and our haulage costs. And sometimes the shortfall is only some small, low-value items like clothes pegs.'*

The factory operates on three seven-hour shifts, Monday to Friday: 105 hours per week, for 50 weeks per year. Regular overtime, typically 15 hours on a Saturday, has been worked most of the last year. Sunday is never used for production, allowing access to machines for routine and major overhauls. Machines are laid out in groups so that each operator can be kept highly utilized, attending to at least four machines. Any product can be made on any machine.

Pierre Dumas, the production manager, was concerned about storage space: *'At the moment our warehouse is full, with products stacked on the floor in every available corner, which makes it vulnerable to damage from passing forklifts and from double-handling. We have finally agreed to approve an extension (costing over one million Euros) to be constructed in June–September this year, which will replace contract warehousing and associated transport which is costing us about 5 per cent of the manufacturing costs of the stored items. The return on investment for this project is well above our current 8 per cent cost of capital. There is no viable alternative, because if we run out of space, production will have to stop for a time. Some of our products occupy very large volumes of rack space. However, in the meantime we have decided to review all the re-order quantities. They seem either to result in excessive stock or too little stock to provide the service required. Large items such as the Baby Bath (Item 143BB) could be looked at first. This is a good starting point because the product has stable and non-seasonal demand. We estimate that it costs us around 20 per cent of the manufacturing variable costs to store such items for one year.'*

Questions

1 Why is TEP unable to deliver all its products reliably within the target of one week, and what effects might that have on the distributors?

2 Applying the EBQ model, what batch size would you recommend for this product? How long will each batch take to produce, and how many batches per year will be made? Should this model be applied to calculate the re-order quantity for all the products, and if not, why?

3 How would the EBQ change if the set-up costs were reduced by 50 per cent, and the holding costs were reassessed at 40 per cent, taking account of the opportunity costs of capital at TEP?

4 What internal problems result from the current planning and control policies? In particular, analyse stock turns and availability (e.g. high and low levels).

5 Using Pareto analysis, categorize the products into Classes A,B,C, based on usage value. Would this approach be useful for categorizing and controlling stock levels of all the products at TEP?

6 What overall recommendations would you make to Francis Lamouche about the proposed investment in the warehouse extension?

CASE
49

Case date
1995

London Zoo

Adrian Watt and Stuart Chambers

Introduction

Dr Jo Gipps, the Director of London Zoo, turned away from his window:

'I have quite a good view of Regents Park and the zoo from here. I can also see the visitors arriving and walking to the main entrance from the car park or the tube station on the other side of the park. You get quite a good feel for the attendance numbers just from watching the stream of people walking along the pavement. By late morning on really busy days we have quite a queue building up at the ticket kiosks. Of course, that doesn't happen as often as it did some years ago, but we would like to see if we could bring the crowds back. We have a huge fluctuation in daily numbers. Our busiest times are obviously weekends and the summer holidays when we regularly get attendance levels of between 4000 and 6000. On the Easter and August Bank Holidays we can easily reach 10 000. The busiest day we have had in the last few years was on a special "Save Our Zoo" day when visitor numbers topped 18 000; the zoo was packed, you could hardly move, the whole operation was bursting at the seams, there were queues everywhere, we were running out of food, it was chaos! Yet our lowest budgeted attendance figure is for Christmas Eve with just 48 people. The place is like a ghost town, it lacks any atmosphere and there are hardly any staff around as they are all getting on with their work behind the scenes.

'We certainly need to increase our visitor numbers, but it is vital that we still provide a high quality of service; and there lies our problem. We have had all the usual market research done for us: we know the age range, group size, average length of visit, where the visitors come from, and even which newspapers they read. We also know which animals they like best: the monkeys, big cats, elephants and penguins are always popular, but we do not really know what the public thinks of the quality of the service we provide throughout their visit. Apart from providing the animals, what are we doing right and when? If we do not know that, how can we improve and build on our successes? Marketing is all very well at getting people here, but once they are here we have to keep them and organise our operations to give them a good day out.

'The second problem is largely concerned with society's attitude to animals, and this is really one of the reasons for the zoo being in the difficulty it is today. The public's views have changed a great deal over the past few years: they have become far more aware of issues such as animal rights and welfare, and conservation, they are far more sceptical of the need to keep animals in captivity, and they are questioning the role of zoos in today's society. London Zoo (and the Zoological Society as a whole including the

Institute of Zoology) has long been primarily dedicated to animal welfare and conservation, but in the past there has been no real need to emphasise this because people did not really seem to care. All they wanted to do was to come to the zoo to see some exotic large animals and did not think about the welfare of the animals in the zoo or the wild. Now things have changed completely! Many people now still want to see the animals, but are worried about their happiness, their well-being and their conservation in their natural habitats. Some people think that zoos are one of the problems rather than part of the solution.

'I suppose this encapsulates our problem; having got the visitors to come, are we treating them well by giving them a good quality service, and indeed are we giving them what they want?'

Background information on London Zoo

Ever since it opened in 1828, London Zoo has played a major part in the country's interest in natural history both as a scientific and recreational activity, and has frequently been in the news headlines. London Zoo is the UK's premier zoological collection and has one of the most prestigious animal collections in the world. It was designed to house and display the 'grand collection of live animals', for the Zoological Society of London. Although initially only occupying a small corner of Regents Park, it expanded rapidly to reach its present size of 36 acres. From the start the zoo had a wide range of exotic species including Indian elephants, llamas, leopards, kangaroos, bears and numerous birds. The collection grew rapidly with the addition of an orangutan, an Indian rhinoceros, giraffes, and chimpanzees all arriving over the next 10 years. The first of a series of gorillas arrived in 1887.

As the collection expanded so building work continued, with major periods of construction and refurbishment occurring in the 1830s, 1850s, 1880s and 1920/30s. For the first 65 years all the animals were permanently housed inside in the mistaken belief that they would not survive the cold outside. The world's first aquarium was built in 1853. The original lion house was replaced in 1876, and the first reptile house which opened in 1849 was replaced in 1883. The existing aquarium was built in 1924, the present reptile house in 1927, the penguin pool in 1934, and the Cotton and Mappin Terraces were also built during the 1930s. The latter are closed awaiting refurbishment, and have been for a number of years. These, and many of the other buildings, are listed and cannot simply be demolished, but must be renovated within strict guidelines.

There was a severe lack of capital investment in the zoo's infrastructure in the 1960s and 1970s. However a spate of building did occur in the 1970s with the Sobell ape and monkey pavilions opening in 1972, followed by the big cat enclosures, and the Snowdon Aviary. In the late 1980s and 1990s there was the redevelopment of the Clore Small Mammal House into the Moonlight Centre and the rebuilding of the Children's and Petting Zoo (which has been present in some form since 1924), the construction of the Lifewatch Centre, Macaw Aviary, and Barclay Court and the fountain area. Recently the zoo has been awarded £2 million from the National Lottery Heritage Millennium Fund to go towards building an education centre.

Visitor attendance levels have always fluctuated as fashion and public interest have increased and waned with the introduction of new exhibits and developments, or as investment declined. In the 1830s annual attendance levels exceeded 250 000, but fluctuated considerably during the latter half of the century. The zoo's popularity increased after the turn of the century with a sustained period of expansion, attendance figures reaching 2 million per annum before the Second World War. After the war, attendance figures leapt to 3 million due to the desire for post-austerity recreation, but by the mid-1950s the visitor numbers had settled back down towards their pre-war 2 million level and remained stable for some time. In the late 1960s and early 1970s a new decline began and by 1975 attendance levels started to fall rapidly. By the early 1980s visitor levels were just over 1 million, and the budgeted 1995/96 attendance level was just 900 000.

This decline in attendance levels was due to a number of socio-economic changes including changing social habits, growth in car ownership, leisure preferences and inflation. In the 1950s there was very little competition from other animal or general leisure attractions. Coupled with this there was a general lack of transport, usually only public transport being available and there being very little private means of transport with only a few cars. This restricted the ability of people who lived in and around London to travel widely beyond the city, or for other people to go anywhere far except to the capital. With the expansion of the road network and increased car ownership, as well as the growth of foreign travel, people found it easier and were more willing to go further for their leisure activities. Competition also grew rapidly with respect to animal based organisations; there were nine zoos in Great Britain in the 1950s but there are now over 250 attractions which include animals. The fastest growing visitor segments were leisure, amusement and country parks. Historical buildings, and the museums and galleries sector remained constant, and wildlife attractions showed the lowest consistent absolute growth, and as a consequence a fall in percentage terms. Thus London Zoo was in a market sector which had a rapidly increasing number of new entrants and competitors, but at the same time its segment was showing a relatively decreasing market size while other visitor attractions expanded rapidly.

The proportional decrease in the attendance of animal attractions was coupled with the change in the public's perception of the rights of animals, the care of animals in captivity and the effect of caging animals on their health, behaviour, and psychology. The morality, function and need of zoos was also questioned with an emphasis being placed on the requirement for conservation to occur in the wild.

Over the last 25 years there has been a general lack of investment in the zoo's infrastructure, new attractions, facilities, educational and conservation development or its image. This occurred just at the time when alternative leisure attractions, both animal based and otherwise, were starting to present substantial competition. The performance of the zoo in the early 1960s to mid-1970s had generated considerable profit which could have been used for the reinvestment in the zoo's infrastructure, but the Zoological Society decided to use the money to support and expand its scientific work at the Institute. In the mid-1970s attendance levels fell sharply and the zoo went into a major financial deficit. At the same time many private donations dried up, and the government was no longer willing to provide money for capital development. A severe money shortage resulted at the very time when capital investment was desperately needed. The zoo reached a desperate position by 1981/82. It was realised that it was imperative to increase gate revenues by developing new exhibits and improving the facilities and the service offered to the public. Between 1985 and 1988 government grants totalled £7.5m, without which the operating deficit would have been £6.5m. In 1988 the zoo applied for £13m for immediate work and £40m for long-term development. The government gave a one-off £10m grant, and informed the zoo that it had to be self-supporting.

Following a number of strategy reports in 1990 the society announced its plans for major changes in the collection. There was a large reduction in the number of species kept, and many animals were moved to its sister collection at Whipsnade in order to reduce costs. Throughout 1991 the zoo produced 80 per cent of its revenue from gate receipts but remained open due to private donations received. Further development plans and fundraising activities took place throughout 1991 and 1992. The incumbent Director of the zoo resigned and was replaced by Dr Jo Gipps, the present Director. Following disappointing attendance levels to early summer 1992, it was announced that the zoo would close by Christmas. However at a special council meeting this decision was reversed by the Fellows, and this was confirmed at the Annual General Meeting in September 1992. A new Council was elected by April 1993.

The 1992 development plan

With the support of the zoo's staff, Dr Gipps' development plan was published and adopted in June 1992. This would cost an estimated £21m over 10 years. The plan focused on the conservation of animals with breeding programmes for endangered species including Asiatic lions, Sumatran tigers, and Lowland gorillas. The aim was summarised in the statement that 'there will be less emphasis on the zoo as a good day out. We are going to appeal to people's intelligence. Zoos have no right to exist in the late 20th century unless they can show they are good for animals.' The plan also detailed the proposed infrastructural changes and reorganisation required as well as the finance required, and the consequences of the changes. Developments were to include a children's zoo, an education centre, the long-term restoration of the dilapidated Mappin Terraces and the reintroduction of the bears. The reorganisation and rationalisation involved the shedding of 90 staff and a reduction in the size of the animal collection, although the remaining animals had enlarged enclosures. An emphasis was placed on cost-cutting and the evaluation of the species in the collection, with particular consideration to those for which the captive breeding programmes were an integral part of their conservation, and in line with the zoo's mission statement.

The 1993/94 period was largely one of financial structural and organisational consolidation after years of upheaval so stabilising and equating income and expenditure and thereby ensuring a secure future that did not exceed income. A new charter and mission statement was ratified in 1994/95. The Zoological Society's mission statement is summarised in Appendix 49.1. There was an organisational restructuring into a series of departments with defined roles and responsibilities. These included the departments for animal management, education, marketing, events, projects, visitor operations, general services and the retail departments, with outside franchises awarded for catering and peripheral visitor activities e.g. face painting. Attendance figures still continued to fall.

Conservation in action

In 1993, in association with the launch of its marketing campaign, summarised by its slogan 'Conservation in Action', London Zoo commissioned its first ever market research poll to establish a visitor profile and to measure the public's awareness of its advertising campaign. This indicated the family and children orientated nature of the visitor profile, that 41 per cent came from London and 14 per cent from overseas. Overall views were positive, with 76 per cent saying that they were likely to return within two years. The decision to visit was largely at the request of the children, was only made a few days prior to the visit, and was strongly influenced by the weather on the day. There was also a high awareness of the zoo and its advertising campaign.

Throughout 1994/95 a small rise was seen in visitor numbers although there was an underlying deficit in revenue of £600 000, offset by a £900 000 private donation. Further market research revealed that the average visit was of four hours, and that the apes and monkeys, big cats, elephants and penguins were the most popular exhibits.

The management of London Zoo

London Zoo consists of eight departments, the heads of which report to Dr Jo Gipps, the Director of London Zoo. The departments consist of the animal management division, marketing, development, general services, projects, retail and visitor operations. In total the zoo directly employs 161 staff. In addition there are catering and other franchise staff employed by outside contractors. The permanent staff are supplemented by temporary staff employed during peak periods such as school and bank holidays. These are largely used at the catering and retail facilities.

The service quality research project

In June 1995, Jo Gipps was addressing a meeting of the monthly management committee:

'For us to manage the budget and to break even we must maintain an attendance level of at least one million visitors a year ... but even then there will be very little money available to carry out the much needed modification of the infrastructure, and the addition of new exhibits. A secure financial future would enable us to carry out our development and expansion plans, and to adapt further as views and perceptions of the public and of society as a whole change. It is therefore essential that we accurately define our target market segments, identify what our customers expect when they come to the zoo, and then provide them with their needs and requirements at a consistently high quality of service. Of course, we must target and attract these customers using accurate and effective marketing, promotions and PR, but to build and maintain a reputation we must be able to deliver what the customers want, or they will not come back. If we fail to do that, the customer will be disgruntled and dissatisfied, and when they return home they will spread their dissatisfaction or disappointment by 'word-of-mouth'. The consequence will be that visitors will not return, and new visitors will not be attracted. If, however, the service is as wanted and expected, or even exceeds expectations, the visitors will leave satisfied and delighted. They will spread the zoo's positive reputation, returning themselves and helping to increase the level of new visitors.

'In order to ensure that we achieve our aim of providing the visitors with an excellent day out and so attract them back again in even greater numbers, it is essential that we find out how they rate their visit. This involves two basic issues: the first is to discover how the zoo performs with respect to the service it provides, and the second is to ensure that it is delivering the services that the customers want. It is only after we have some measure of these things that we can hope to fine tune our operating procedures, and develop a plan of action to tackle problem areas in some order of priority. I have decided to seize an opportunity to use an MBA student, Adrian Watt, to undertake a major customer research programme over this summer, so I hope you will all find the time to assist him when necessary. His work should give us a much better understanding of what we must do, but first it is important to ensure that an accurately defined segment of visitors is targeted. We have three general categories of visitors: school and education groups; large parties and coach trips; and individuals, couples or family groups. Each category requires different services from the zoo during their visit. The latter group represents our largest category of visitors, particularly during the summer months, so Adrian should only target these this year. Overseas visitors can be included as long as they are fluent in English, because they account for about 15 per cent of the total visitors, and could provide us with a valuable means of international competitive benchmarking. Perhaps Adrian could explain to you all how he intends to go about his project?'

Designing a questionnaire

Adrian explained that he would first need their help in designing the questionnaire:

'What I would like to do is to use a list of the "18 determinants of service quality" [see Appendix 49.2] as a guideline for the design of the questionnaire. I would like you all to help me translate these into a comprehensive list of appropriate questions that we could ask about the zoo and the visitors' day here. We should word them so that people can make a judgement of their perceptions of the quality of the service they have experienced, on a 1 to 5 scale, where 1 is very bad and 5 is very good, and hence 3 is average. The scores will then be analysed using statistical software.

'It is essential that our questions also reflect the areas that are relevant and of importance to the zoo, and that are within the control of the zoo, so that you can act to alter or influence the provision of the quality of those aspects of the service. It is equally important that the questions are not ambiguous, too complex, or leading. Consequently the wording must be kept simple and the phraseology might use terms such as "how did you rate" to avoid leading statements such as "how good" or "how bad", which may influence the respondents' rating score.

'Having ascertained how the visitors perceive the quality of the service the zoo provides, the second part of the questionnaire will be designed to discover what customers expected from the zoo during their visit. This can be achieved by providing a list of short statements derived from each of the questions asked in the first section of the questionnaire. Each statement will be a non-committal sentence which does not indicate that this is the standard actually provided by London Zoo, but rather it is a desired standard that should be provided. The respondent will be asked to consider their expectations of the zoo, and to select and rank the top ten statements. This would enable us to obtain an indication of exactly what visitors wanted from their visit to the zoo.'

After several attempts at designing the questionnaire, including a reduction in the number of questions to manageable levels, a final version was agreed (see Appendix 49.3). It was necessary for visitors to have experienced a large proportion of the zoo's facilities and service process, as a result all respondents had to have been at the zoo for at least two hours prior to the interview (half the average visit duration) in order to be allowed to complete a questionnaire, assisted by Adrian. As a result, interviewing only started after 12.30 p.m. on any given day so that visitors could have been at the zoo for the requisite time, and interviewing continued until 5.30 p.m. when the zoo closed. Because each interview took approximately 15 minutes, it was considered necessary to approach potential interviewees who were already resting, as would often be the case for visitors who had already been at the zoo for two hours.

As a result the areas used to select potential respondents were predominately those in which people were likely to be resting and eating, namely seating areas and near to the restaurant and cafe facilities.

The interviews were conducted on a group basis with all members of the group taking part. It was stressed that the questions should be answered with respect to the group as a whole. For example, the visibility of the animals would include a child's ability to see as well as an adult. Access would include the ability to gain access for those with pushchairs and small children or elderly people as well as adults. Other questions involving perceptions were usually answered following a discussion which gave rise to a consensus; if a strong divergence of views occurred, which was rare within a group, either those with the strongest (not necessarily the most extreme views) or a majority vote usually prevailed. A consensus group view was also obtained for the second part of the questionnaire to obtain a top ten priority ranking of those aspects of the visit that they felt the zoo should provide.

The expected subjective variability of the responses that would be obtained, required a large sample size over a broad range of attendance levels. The survey was carried out over the summer months of July, August and September 1995. This included the school summer holidays, a bank holiday and a pre and post-holiday period. This would sample a wide range of attendances, which were predicted to be between 1000 and 9500 visitors per day. The sample days selected reflected this range. The size of the overall sample was therefore determined by the fact that each individual day had to have a potentially statistical credible size group, the size only being limited by the number of people that could be questioned on any given day. The target number of completed questionnaires per day was 20.

Having agreed the design of the questionnaire, and selected the appropriate segment of visitors for interviewees, the range of sample days, the sample times and other criteria, Dr Gipps concluded:

'All our previous market research has been on a very different track. We know a great deal about our visitors' demographics, where they come from, and the newspapers they read. However, I can now appreciate that we didn't find out anything about what they thought about their visit, or how we performed in giving them a good day out, nor what they actually wanted or expected from us or their visit in the first place. The one commonality with Adrian's work is that we also carried out the survey on a wide range of days from the slowest to almost the busiest, so that when we averaged the results we got a really representative view of the average visitor on an average day. The only days we didn't survey were the really busy ones, because we felt that it might only add to any problems. If people were tired due to queues and the general bustle, the last thing they would want to do was answer a list of questions!'

Results

Over the three-month period of the survey (July, August and September 1995), a total of 755 questionnaires were completed on 38 separate days. The first was carried out on 20 July before the school summer holidays had begun, and the last on 18 September after the schools had gone back. The attendance levels varied between 1046 on 18 September and 9554 on the August Bank Holiday Monday. The total number of people to visit the zoo on these days was 183 395, with an average daily attendance level of 4826 visitors. The mean group size was 3.6 with a modal group size of 4. This represented mainly family parties, and of these a mean of 1.9 or 43 per cent of all visitors were children under 16. Most people arrived between 11.00 a.m. and 12.29 p.m., and the mean visit time was four hours 50 minutes. The weather was consistently excellent during the entire research period, as the UK experienced one of its hottest and driest summers on record.

The results for the performance and priority sections of the survey were digitised and fed into a spreadsheet in order to analyse the huge quantity of data, using a combination of standard and specially written software. The results were analysed and the scores scaled onto a 1 to 5 scale, with 1 representing the poorest performance or of very low priority, and 5 representing an excellent performance or the highest priority to be provided by the zoo. This scaling was simple for the performance ratings as the visitor had already awarded a score of 1 to 5, and so the final rating was simply an average of the scores achieved for each day or appropriate attendance band. The scaling of the priorities assigned to each aspect of a visit was more complex. The priorities were given as rankings and were therefore relative. Each priority ranking was assigned a score with the highest priority (1) receiving the highest score, the lowest priority (10) receiving the lowest score, and all those not included in the top ten list were given a score of zero. All the scores assigned to any given aspect were added together for any given day or attendance band, and these were then ranked in order of scores, with the highest overall score representing the highest overall priority. To scale these scores onto a 1 and 5 scale, the highest score achieved by any aspect in any attendance band was awarded a score of 5, and then all the other scores were scaled by the same factor to achieve a score between 0 and 5. As only the highest score achieved in any set of attendance bands was awarded a 5 it enabled a true comparison to be made between attendance bands, to see how priorities changed under different conditions.

The results were collected and presented in four categories:

1 The overall results averaged for all the data sets obtained
2 The data divided into three groups of daily visitor attendance levels:
   - 0 to 2999 visitors per day;
   - 3000 to 5999 visitors per day;
   - over 6000 visitors per day.

The performance and priority results are tabulated in Appendix 49.4 and 49.5 respectively.

At first sight the data appeared to show that the zoo was performing well overall, although there was significant variation between different attributes of quality. Also, as could be expected, there was a wide variation in the priority rankings with some factors scoring almost a maximum score of 5, and others only a quarter of that.

Adrian's task was the interpretation and use of the data to help the zoo's management derive some idea of how it was performing in providing visitors with a good day out and where it was failing to provide a reasonable quality of service, and under what conditions this occurred. He would have to summarise the visitors' rankings of the zoo's performance and of what they expected from the zoo. And finally he would have to help the zoo determine a prioritised plan of action to improve its service delivery system.

Questions

1 (a) *Using the 18 determinants of service quality, devise your own questionnaire for the zoo. Compare your questionnaire to the one actually used.*

   (b) *Which determinants of service quality are investigated by which question?*

2 *What do the various sets of figures tell you about the zoo's performance from the visitors' perspective? In which are the zoo performing best of all, and where are the areas of poor performance? Which areas and type of the operational processes do they reflect? How and why do they vary?*

3 *Do the visitors' priorities vary in a similar manner and why?*

4 *Derive a plan of action and priority list which will help the zoo decide which aspects of its service provision to tackle first. What factors may need to be taken into account while formulating this order of action?*

5 *Evaluate the strengths and weaknesses of the questionnaire in its objective of providing a priority agenda for improvement to operations.*

East State Hospital

This case is based on a real organisation and was written by Professor Robert Johnston, Warwick Business School, 2012. All names and places have been changed.

Anita Rashid is a senior nurse at the East State Hospital. She explained the problem she was facing after two years in post as Lead Nurse Specialist for the Patient Experience: "We have been working really hard to improve the patient's experience in our hospital, but the statistics tell us that the patient experience has not improved at all. Worse still our staff seem to resent us talking to them about it. They get quite antagonistic when we give them the feedback from patients. I really don't know what more I can do to make a difference.

"We have to undertake patient surveys because we have to capture and report statistics to management and also the government. However, we do realise that these surveys don't help us understand what the causes of the problems are; they just provide numbers and trends. So we collect a lot of information that really helps us understand what is actually going on. We do face-to-face and telephone interviews with patients, their relatives or carers, and members of the public. We invite groups of past patients in and get them telling stories about their experiences with us, the good and the bad. We get a proportion of patients to keep diaries during their stay in hospital, writing down the things they notice. We even have comment cards available on the wards which we also analyse.

"Of course we are most concerned about the outcome of care the patient receives and we have many processes and protocols in place to try to ensure the best outcomes for our patients. However, I am concerned about the patient's experience; their journey through the service and how they feel about what happens to them. We all have to follow medical processes and protocols but we should also be thinking about the experience the patient is undergoing – i.e. how does it feel from a patient's point of view.

"From our analysis we have identified a number of feelings that patients want and expect including safe, cared for, respected and compassion. We have then defined these in terms that can be understood by both patients and staff. For example safe means not getting an infection, having staff around, and feeling like people will respond to requests in good time. Feeling cared for includes knowing the patient's name and using it as they wish to be called, when staff say they will be back in a minute, actually being back in a minute, and importantly being recognised and treated as a person rather than the hernia in bed four!

"We used to write out an action plan for each complaint we received and report back to the person who sent it, thanking them and telling them what we planned to do to change things or occasionally explaining why we were unable to change things. We would also check that any changes had been made. However, our CEO has recently told us that we should only create action plans and respond to patients about major problems or incidents. We still send a report to each division every month with a summary of the complaints, the trends and the key issues. We even use process control charts for the number of complaints. We will also add in any information from patients' diaries or what the patient panels have told us. We often refer to these as LTMs - 'little things that matter'. For example, one patient complained that the nurses always asked how his leg was and how the operation went but they never asked 'how are you'? Another comment was about when nurses take the patient's temperature, they just walk away saying 'it's fine', whereas most patients want to know what the temperature was – in numbers. Patients and visitors also want to be acknowledged as they walk on to the ward past the nursing station. So we are trying to teach the nurses to look up, even if they are on the phone, make eye contact and say, 'be with you in a moment' or whatever. It's these little things that we want to get the staff to think about. Improving the patient's experience can be really simple by just dealing with these little things. Staff need to realise that they can easily make a big difference with very little time or effort.

"The problem is in getting them to do these things. We have senior nurses who go on to the wards to check that all these things are happening as well as senior managers who occasionally visit and check what's happening on the wards. We run patient experience training courses and every member of staff has to attend one each year although some people seem to resent it; they just want to get on with the job. It's also very difficult when we give staff the feedback from patients, whether directly or in the training sessions. They immediately explain that whatever it is couldn't possibly happen on their ward. When we give them the facts that whatever it was did happen, they then explain the reasons behind it, such as they were too busy, or there was an emergency, or they were short staffed, or noone has ever complained before. They can get quite antagonistic because they assume you are accusing them of not caring. The problem is they all believe they are doing a good job. They say 'I am working as hard as I can; doing my best and now you are telling me I am not doing it right'. They just don't seem to realise that many of the things they are doing are creating a poor experience for patients."

Implementing lean at CWHT

by Nicola Burgess, Warwick University

In July 2011, the acting Chief Executive of Chaswick and Wallasey NHS Hospital Trust (CWHT) took the decision to implement lean thinking across the organisation. The idea was to bring the hospital into line with other hospitals in the UK where lean improvement initiatives were becoming increasingly widespread. In fact, the trust had started to experiment with lean principles two years earlier. The external consultants used for this initial work were not asked to bid for the new initiative. Despite their global reputation for world-class engineering it was felt that the previous lean work had been disjointed, fragmented and too focused on the need to optimise departments around targets. This time the trust wanted a much more coherent and joined up approach to lean implementation. This time they were thinking about 'transformation' into becoming a total *lean organisation*. All the consultants who were bidding for the contract emphasised building 'soft skills' training and 'project facilitation' that would equip the organisation with an internal change team capable of rolling out lean throughout the hospital. The internal change team was led by a 'Head of Lean' and several Lean Leaders, many of whom joined the team as part of a secondment from their clinical roles. The 'Lean team' comprised 11 staff employed on two-year contracts.

During the period September–December 2011, preparations for implementing lean throughout the trust took place led by the external consultants who had won the contract: 'Change M'. Eighteen projects were designed to take place across three streams of work to reflect a number of patient pathways throughout the organisation. The aim was to move staff out of their functional 'silos' and to help them see their role within the whole patient pathway rather than within a single function. Meanwhile, the lean facilitators underwent training in project facilitation and change management skills. The project roll-out was set to begin January 2012.

A new Chief Executive

In October 2011 a new Chief Executive Sir William Oberon was appointed to begin work in January. He had an impressive record, with Chief Executive roles at a number of hospitals, including a world-leading heart specialist hospital, and had overseen successful turnarounds in two of the worst performing hospitals in England. Following his appointment, Sir William immediately instructed

Source: Alex Segre/Alamy Images

consultants TOC-Health (with whom he had worked in the past) to enter CWHT in December 2011 and begin work straight away in the Accident and Emergency (A&E) department. A new Director of Operations also began in post in December 2011. This made the assignment difficult for TOC-Health. Adam Smith, Client Director of TOC-Health explained: *'It was a funny situation really. We arrived in the Trust before William had taken up his appointment and before the new Director of Operations. We had to introduce ourselves to the Lean Team. It was rather embarrassing and awkward, but William had said: "I want it done very quickly Adam". It's not usually the way we work.'*

TOC-Health had been employed with very clear responsibility to sort out problems in A&E. The Lean Team had been asked to steer clear of the work. At the time UK healthcare targets specified that 98 per cent of patients must be seen within four hours of arrival and so CWHT had implemented a new Clinical Decision Unit (CDU) to help expedite people out of A&E so as not to breach the target. Unfortunately, at the end of 2011, the Trust was still operating at around 95 per cent which meant that the trust would not obtain a good performance rating. In addition, the trust had a large number of patient outliers (patients in the wrong beds, on the wrong wards) and some financial overruns. In addition they were also struggling on other important targets. Speaking about Sir William's decision to take on the Chief Executive role, the Director of TOC-Health quoted Sir William's words: *'CWHT has this fantastic new building, it's just ridiculous it's not meeting it targets. The hospital is punching well below its weight – the size of the prize is huge!'*

Approaches to improvement

Talking about the approach of TOC-Health, their Director explained: *'The whole point about our approach is fast, focused breakthroughs in performance. You must identify the one true bottleneck and focus on fixing that. In our opinion, if you improve process by process you are chasing your tail, you're just never going to get there; it will take you so long that by the time you've improved, it will have changed anyway.'* It soon became clear that the two consultancy firms had very different approaches to the number of improvement projects that should run concurrently. TOC-Health was focused around the idea that an organisation should not have many disparate projects on the go simultaneously, rather they should focus on just one (the bottleneck). Change M, on the other hand were happy to let many projects take place in various parts of the organisation using what they called the Rapid Improvement Event (RIE) approach.

Meanwhile, although the Head of Lean had begun her projects on schedule, the instruction to keep away from A&E where TOC-Health was working meant her planned activities had to be rescheduled. Nor was she happy with the changes in responsibilities. *'I think we had a reasonably clear understanding of how lean would be implemented until we had a change of Chief Executive. I now feel we don't have a clear way forward to becoming a lean organisation. The emphasis has shifted to get some events done and get some money out; that isn't what lean is about.'* Similar concerns had been expressed about how to measure the success and benefits of the Lean Team. *'Again the emphasis has shifted. Originally it was about having a positive impact, getting people involved in lean, engaging and empowering them towards continuous improvement and following a set of key principles, but now it's changed to "save some money", and people are forgetting the cultural side of it.'*

The 'principles' that the Head of Lean was referring to had been adapted from the lessons learned from lean practitioners in healthcare.* The main principles were as follows:

1 Focus on the patient (not the organisation and its employees, suppliers, etc.) and design care around them in order to determine what real value represents.
2 Identify what represents value for the patient (along the whole value stream or patient pathway) and get rid of everything else.
3 Reduce the time required to go from start to finish along every pathway (which creates more value at less cost).

4 Pursue principles 1, 2, and 3 endlessly through continuous improvement that engages everyone (doctors, nurses, technicians, managers, suppliers, and patients and their families) who 'touch' the patient pathways.

A new arrival

In February, and much to the Head of Lean's surprise, a third set of consultants was appointed to focus on the application of Work Study Method to operating theatres. *'I think the timescales have changed. Before, there was a recognition that we're in it for the long haul, it wasn't going to be a quick fix. I think now the driver is that "you will become a high performing trust come hell or high water and if what we need to do to get there is to bring a hundred management consultants in who've all got a different approach then that's what we'll do". My worry is that in the longer term we'll fall over again because actually all we've done is stick sticking plaster over again which is what we were doing before.'*

The impact of lean

Consultants and nurses in the trust were divided on the impact of lean. Those who had experienced Change M's rapid improvement events (RIEs) in their area tended to be enthusiastic about the benefits and the changes they had made. Small, but significant, changes could produce benefits including reduced confusion, increased staff morale and better patient flow. For example, improved prominence and clarity of signage stopped patients getting lost, and leaving clinicians to wait for them. A reduction in stock levels produced cost and space savings as well as reducing the amount of time spent looking for the correct items. In one store cupboard 25,000 pairs of surgical gloves were identified from 500 different suppliers. Another RIE blew the myth on the effectiveness of the Medical Records Department: *'It was amazing. We just exploded the myth that when you didn't get case notes in a clinical area it was medical records fault, but it hardly ever was. Consultants had notes in their cars, they had them at home, we had a thousand notes in the secretary's offices, and we wondered why we couldn't get case notes! Two people walked seven miles a day looking for them – they were all over the place. Now that was a good RIE because we did manage to sort out medical records and create some semblance of order in their lives.'*

Yet those who had no direct involvement in the lean activity are sceptical: *'We're not making cars, people are different and the processes that we put people through repeatedly are more complicated than the processes that you go through to make a car. These ideas may be OK in manufacturing, but all it has resulted in here are teams of expensive consultants crawling all over the hospital'* (Consultant Surgeon). But there were some converts

*Particularly a book called *On the Mend* by John Toussaint and Roger Gerard (www.onthemendbook.org)

according to the Head of Lean. '*A consultant (medical) came to me at the beginning of the week saying, "This is all a load of rubbish. There's no point in mapping the process, we all know what happens: the patient goes from there to there and this is the solution and this is what we need to do". During the middle of the improvement week, the Consultant said: "I never realised what actually does happen in reality." By the end of the week the Consultant's mindset has changed to: "Actually this has been great because I never understood, I only saw my bit of it".*'

Although frustrated by the confusion caused by using multiple consultants, the Head of Lean was optimistic. '*We are starting to see some quite significant, if limited, results. The real issue is getting everyone to change the way they behave. It is tackling doctors who are used to doing their own thing and having no performance measures. It is negotiating with suppliers familiar with a culture that allows them to offer new apparatus with little attention to cost or clinical benefits. It is gradually persuading nurses that constantly working around problems*

in the care delivery process will not make deep-seated problems go away. It is slowly educating administrators to accept that that you cannot simply run broken processes harder. Ultimately we have seen that lean can potentially work in healthcare. What we have yet to discover is a method for communicating the benefits and value of lean to others, and quantifying this value in a manner that is significant at an executive level of the organisation.'

QUESTIONS

1 What complexities and barriers to lean implementation are demonstrated in the case study?

2 How do the complexities and barriers identified above relate to your own organisation?

3 How might an organisation overcome these barriers?

Case Exercise   Cranleigh Metropolitan Council

Robert Johnston, Warwick Business School, and Zoe Radnor, Cardiff Business School, with the help of Gio Bucci, AtoZ Business Consultancy

Cranleigh Metropolitan Council (CMC) serves a local population of over 350,000 and employs around 14,000 members of staff within seven directorates (departments): Chief Executive's Office, Children's Services, Education & Community Services, Housing, Urban Environment, Law & Property, and Finance. CMC was amongst the top performing local authorities in the country, yet Chief Executive Maeve Andrews was keen to improve the service it provided. She explained the opportunity she saw:

> CMC provides several hundred services for our customers all of which have many different access points, in different buildings with different opening times and using different systems. For example, Housing Services are in one building, Finance, where you pay your bills, in another and benefit payments (part of Finance) in three others. So anyone wanting, as many people do, to access several services at once have to trail around the city, only then to get referred to another department somewhere else. We also have over 100 different telephone numbers – how is a customer meant to know which is the right one? We have decided we want to create one point of contact, a one-stop-shop, where we can bring all our services together and do as much for the customer at the first point of contact. This will make things much better for the customer and should also create important efficiency savings for CMC.

The Council seconded Tony Templeton from a firm of transformation consultants to lead an internal team to see if such a concept was feasible, and if it was, to construct an implementation plan. Tony and the small transformation team – four analysts, three technical developers and an implementation support manager – worked well together and quickly established a compelling case for the implementation of a one-stop-shop. The Council gave the go-ahead and provided a large two-storey building right in the heart of the city to become the new one-stop-shop, to be known as Cranleigh Central. The team quickly developed a plan for bringing services together at one point. Senior analyst Sameer Godhwani explained their approach:

> We try and follow a standard methodology, basically a lean approach, but we have to be flexible to the needs of each area, basically to ensure we keep the Heads of the various directorates on board. The first thing we do is draw up the scoping document, get it agreed and signed off by the directorate involved.

The scoping document identifies the key members of staff involved, the service areas that need to be covered by the investigation and the resources the directorate would need to commit to the transfer to Cranleigh Central. The team then assesses the existing service to get to know the key players and processes, to understand what will be affected by the change and to identify the current effort that is expended by the directorate delivering the service. They analyse the existing process documentation, look at volumes and observe timings. They then map the process, focusing on inputs, outputs, barriers and enablers. One key objective of this stage is to get the agreement of all those involved. Tony added:

> We try to agree on where things are not being done efficiently and where they don't add value for the customer. We sometimes hold workshops and focus groups with customers to identify problems and solutions from their point of view too. The scoping document then has to be signed off by the directorate. We then develop a design for the new service to be based in Cranleigh Central. We test the ideas with the key players and prepare a proposal, setting out the processes to be moved to Central, the costs and benefits, and the budget to be transferred from the directorate involved to Central. Once the design document is completed, it is signed off by the head of the directorate and the head of Cranleigh Central. Some existing staff may be selected to move to Central; we entice them with slightly higher pay. Sometimes new staff are hired to run the new processes in the one-stop-shop. We then thoroughly test all the systems to ensure that what has been developed matches the design. Once the analysts are happy, my team arranges for a demonstration to both the directorate's staff and Central's staff to get the project signed off by those involved. We embark on further testing, create any necessary publicity for the public and then we go live with

that service. The fastest design has been three weeks, the longest took 15 months. Generally the length of the process is dependent upon lots of factors including size of directorate, willingness, commitment and range of services etc.

However, it's not been easy bringing about change. Obviously we have to spend a lot of time with the people who are directly affected by what we come up with and it takes a lot of time and patience to get them on board, especially when their jobs are affected. Even when the transfer is seen as a good idea and the directorate work with us in partnership mode, it can still be quite painful dealing with all the issues. We have to rely on our soft skills. And, it's not becoming easier either. In fact as we start to move into some of the areas which really don't want to be part of this, it will become more difficult. So far we have only worked with areas that have been more receptive.

We started off being careful to work only with directorates that were keen and interested in the one-stop-shop concept. We really wanted to focus on high volume, low complexity and telephone-based services, but in fact we worked with any directorate that was interested. While the main motivations for inclusion into Cranleigh Central were that the service would be better for the customer and it would lead to overall efficiencies, some directors were less willing than others for us to evaluate their services. Some people are a bit precious about their services. It's not always easy getting them to commit to change.

The team has encountered some resistance to get some directorates involved in the transfer of services, in particular through fear of job losses. Indeed the shift in services to Cranleigh Central has resulted in job losses in some areas. And where there has been a reduction in costs it is not seen as an actual saving in the directorate because they have lost part of their budget, and responsibility, to Central.

Two years after the start of implementation Cranleigh Central opened with a blaze of publicity. Employing around fifty people, it quickly became a convenient, friendly and accessible customer contact point for many of the Council's services. It has long opening hours. It has its own call centre (able to deal with a wide range of queries) located on the first floor and accessed by one telephone number. There is a website and email address for queries too. It also has its own walk-in centre on the ground floor. This is a large, spacious, modern-looking building with large glass doors leading towards a reception area. In the area beyond reception are located cash machines for paying Council bills, private rooms for conversations with advisors, and computers providing free internet access. Residents can, for example, pay their tax bills, report faulty street lights or missed bin collections, report abandoned vehicles, pay housing bills and even register births and deaths. It also provides access to other services such as Age Concern and the Citizens Advice Bureau as well as other public sector and community agencies such as local transport and tourist information.

Although some of the front-office operations from three of the directorates, such as reporting faulty street lights, are now centralised at Cranleigh Central, the back-office operations, such as mending the faulty lights, are still delivered by the directorates involved. Central simply passes the information they receive to the appropriate team in the appropriate directorate.

Two years and six months into the implementation phase, Maeve Andrews suddenly announced that no further services would be moved to Central and that a review would be undertaken of the work so far. She even hinted that one possible outcome might include the closure of Cranleigh Central. Tony was furious. He explained:

The satisfaction scores of all the services we have moved have gone through the roof and even with the set-up costs, such as staffing costs, software development, hiring and training costs of Central, we have managed to break even in the first twelve months. We are also projecting a £10 million saving next year and double that in the following year. We feel like we have been stabbed in the back.

Questions

1   Is the approach taken a 'lean approach' as claimed?

2   Why do you think the project is in danger?

3   What could Tony and his team have done differently?

CASE STUDY — The National Tax Service (NTS)[14]

The National Tax Service (NTS) was the government agency that assessed and collected taxes from citizens and businesses. The organization was committed to providing an excellent service by applying the tax laws fairly and making it simple and convenient for their 'customers' to fulfil their tax obligations. Its staff aimed to be polite, prompt, competent, clear and consistent. The NTS had a set of service standards including answering 85 per cent of calls within 1 minute, replying to 80 per cent of emails within 5 working days and processing refunds within 30 days. In return it expected its customers to complete their tax returns promptly, give accurate and complete information, keep proper records and pay their tax on time.

Despite the organization's success in meeting its service standards, Max Serwotka, director of the NTS, explained his reasons for initiating the Lean Programme: 'We are

under pressure from the government not only to make substantial cost savings but also improve the service we provide to citizens and businesses. I attended a lean workshop some time ago and I reckon the principles of lean and its benefits could be applied directly to us. So I appointed a lean consultancy to help us implement a Lean Programme. They informed me that a Lean Programme should be able to deliver, within 12 months, a 30 per cent improvement in productivity, reduce backlogs and improve consistency in our processing capabilities, and improve the customer experience. They recommended a three-step approach: first, redesign our service delivery processes to eliminate waste and variability; second, change management processes to create a structure that will help implement and sustain improvements; and third, change the mindsets of leaders and front-line staff to support the new systems and deliver continuous improvement.'

The consultants began by running a number of events including start-up events (SUE) with senior managers to explain the principles of lean, the approach to be taken and to establish an operational performance focus, as well as a series of two-day performance improvement events (PIE) for front-line staff to engage them in the process and identify the first set of issues to work on. These were followed by task team events (TTE) where task teams were set up, facilitated by the consultants, to focus on a few of the issues that were raised. These events were rolled out rapidly across the organization and supported with a number of workshops aimed at giving the members of the task teams skills

in a number of techniques, including process-mapping, problem-solving, waste identification and project management. The objective was to make the Lean Programme self-sustaining within one year.

The initial response to the programme was extremely positive, as one senior manager related: 'For a long time the NTS has been focused on staff and things like hours of working and flexibility of hours; we have always looked at it from a staff perspective. Under the Lean Programme we are looking at things from a customer perspective. The aim is to deal immediately with customers' tax returns and queries and meet the government's "demand" for tax revenues from us, with no problems or errors, at minimum cost. Although we set the deadlines for tax returns and payments, our customers should set the pace and initiate the flow of activities.'

Within six months of the start of the Programme members of staff seemed to be less than enthusiastic. Comments from front-line staff included: 'We went to a workshop where we did an exercise with bits of paper and coloured dots, making "products" from them to meet requests from "customers". It was all good fun and we all enjoyed it. But it didn't work when we came back to our desks. We do our jobs differently because every tax return is different. We can't see the principles working here.' And 'Lean can't work in a tax office. The consultants have worked in manufacturing and in hospitals, but not a tax office.'

Max had good contacts with the local university and asked Professor Kaz Khalid and her team to assess how well the Lean Programme was going. Within a few months the team had visited 10 tax offices, 3 regional processing centres and the central processing centre. They interviewed 137 staff, including senior managers and front-line staff, to gain an understanding of what they thought of the Lean Programme, what its aims were and how well it had succeeded in meeting those aims. Their conclusion was that even though the Lean Programme had made an impact there were significant issues that still needed to be addressed. This presented a new set of challenges for Max. Their report stated: 'The Lean Programme has engaged and challenged people but it is not the foundation for lean that it was designed to be. The Programme is not applying all the principles of lean, and the NTS has a considerable way to go before it can describe itself as a lean organization. However, this does not mean that "Lean" is not working; there has been a movement in the right direction, but it has a considerable way to go.' The team's key findings included:

- Senior managers don't appear to be engaged with the Programme, though they appear to understand the nature of lean and the Lean Programme much better than the front-line staff.
- While some processes and practices have been modified and made clearer, there have been only marginal benefits in terms of productivity and the customer experience.
- The focus of the task teams appears to have been mainly concerned with waste reduction rather than a focus on the customer; indeed there has been no consultation or involvement with customers and key stakeholders.
- A few areas have seen improvements in productivity but these have not been shared with other parts of the organization.
- Many of the key processes were seen to be 'centrally owned' so staff felt they were unable to influence them.
- Staff seem to welcome the workshops and the problem-solving skills they were developing but they voiced frustration that when they made suggestions they were not followed through.

Some of the quotes contained in the report were as follows:

'The improvements were supposedly going to be massive and many of the senior managers thought changes would be very difficult to implement, knowing how the organization worked. Then negativity crept in with managers and staff, and so the improvements didn't actually come about.'

'There isn't much support from the consultants. We analyse problems and make suggestions but there doesn't seem to be any way of making the changes.'

'A lot of front-line staff seemed worried about joining the task teams. There was a view that jobs might be at risk.'

'We have heard about this lean initiative but we have not been consulted or involved.'

'We heard that one of the sites had made some changes and removed some waste, but it had upset so many taxpayers that they had changed things back. We started to be worried about making any changes.'

'We have daily meetings now but they don't seem to serve any purpose. We discuss targets and quality, but most of the time we talk about things we got wrong.'

'How can we move to a "pull" system when we have such a big backlog of work?'

'The targets are simply not achievable. We can never succeed whatever we do.'

However, there had been some successes. The introduction of quality managers had helped identify problems and errors early and help staff better understand what to do. Managers also indicated that the Programme was helping them identify those in the team who worked well and those who were struggling. At three of the sites, managers mentioned that teamworking had improved, with teams becoming more integrated, with a better team spirit because they better understood the processes they were involved in. The removal of waste had also had some success at a few sites with non-value-adding elements of some processes being removed. In terms of customer focus the senior managers referred to 'the customer' and understood the need to deliver better service. However, many members of the front-line staff were struggling with the notion of 'the customer'. Some quotes were as follows:

'We find it difficult to understand "the customer". We don't actually use the word but we hear it more often now.'

'We deal with bits of paper not customers.'

'We never see the customer and most people don't even talk to a customer, so it's just a bit of paper or a screen. Sometimes we forget that there is a customer at the other end.'

'The taxpayers are told they have to pay. We are supposed to call them customers, but they're not.'

'We have more of a realization about customer focus than we ever had. I am not saying that we are there yet, but we are getting there.'

Max summarized his views. *'Since the start of the programme productivity has hardly increased; we still have the same backlog of work. However, quality has improved a little. There are now many more quality checks during the process with dedicated quality managers doing the checking. Now feedback on errors and problems is much faster so staff are now learning from their mistakes. From the point of view of our customers, things must have got better. However, we are a long, long way from achieving what this Programme set out to achieve. I was taught that there are three key stages to lean; engage, establish and embed. Far from engaging our staff we appear to have alienated some of them. Questions are now being asked by members of the government about the costs and benefits of the Lean Programme and my head is on the line.'*

CASE
33

Case date
2001

The Smart Car and smart logistics

© Remko van Hoek and Alan Harrison

At the beginning of October 1998 most of the parking places in downtown Amsterdam were filled with one or ... two cars. The variety in colours and the remarkable design of the two-seater car attracted great attention. The message was clear: Smart had come to town and it's here to revolutionise the concept of car production, logistics and marketing.

Micro Compact Car AG (MCC), a wholly-owned subsidiary of Daimler-Benz (formerly a joint venture of Daimler-Benz and Swatch), is the company behind Smart. Together these manufacturers have developed what they call a new mobility concept that relieves the heavy environmental pressure caused by present traffic while still ensuring continuous individual mobility. Overlooking the period preceding the introduction of the car, MCC management could look back on many peaks: a completely new brand had been developed; pilot marketing of brand and product concept had raised high levels of customer awareness and interest in European markets; a production site of 68 hectares had been developed and constructed from scratch; a dealer and marketing organisation had been developed and was ready for product launch. Moreover, the supply chain concept developed went beyond existing practices in the automotive industry on a number of points:

- Customers can say how they want their product to be configured
- Lead-times for cars are counted in weeks
- Suppliers have co-invested in the production location and take a greater share in the final assembly process
- The value added during final assembly is just 10 per cent of the production cost price
- Supplier facilities are integrated in the assembly hall of MCC.

From the time of the first feasibility study by Mercedes in 1993 and the foundation of MCC in 1994, the management team realised it was facing a new set of challenges in terms of developing and integrating the supply chain. How should the supply chain be managed, coordinated, controlled and further developed? These questions were not only of relevance to MCC, but to the Daimler-Benz Corporation as a whole, which earmarked Smart as a strategic learning project. Moreover, the concept being brought to practice by MCC is widely considered by leading car manufacturers as of key importance to future industry developments. Manufacturers and suppliers therefore monitor the successes and failures of MCC, as the results will in future influence organisation of many other supply chains.

Figure 33.1 The Smart City Coupé

The car

The Smart City Coupé is a two-seater car measuring 2.5 metres in length, 1.51 metres in width and 1.53 metres in height (Figure 33.1). It has been developed mainly for in-city use. It's a safe and environment-friendly car; despite its micro credentials, it combines driver comfort, safety and customer choice. According to MCC, the car is an answer to mobility problems in urban areas. A key target was to minimise the burden on the environment caused by individual mobility. By using changeable body parts, the life cycle of the car can be extended. Moreover, the car and its components are fully recyclable after use. Its size also makes it friendly to the environment, as it needs a relatively small and fuel-efficient engine – and two Smarts can be parked in a single parking slot.

The Smart is based on a rigid integral body frame/safety cell (called 'Tridion'), to which such flexible body panels as doors, the front and rear panels and the optional glass roof are attached. The customer can specify the product by combining two colours of the frame (black and silver) with the various colours of the body panels. This way the customer is given the impression of a high level of choice, although product variation in the production process is kept to a minimum.

Product variations differ in interior trim, body colours, comfort features and engine power. The modular product layout enables MCC to supply customer choice with minimum product complexity. As most of the features are easy to add, both at the assembly line and during the life span of the car, variation in customer demand hardly interferes with production processes. For example, the interior trim (fabric and colour) consists of exchangeable panels, easy to mount at the assembly line and even easy to be exchanged by the owner afterwards. Moreover, features that might disturb production, if made optional (such as ABS, electric windows, etc.), are integrated as standards in the car. The after-sales extras include a wide range of easy-to-attach peripherals such as stereo and children's seats.

On top of this customisation, the modular concept enables the customer completely to renew and upgrade the product during its lifetime. Product features can be added and coloured body parts can be changed in the dealership (called the 'Smart Centre').

Moreover, the modular concept makes it possible for designers and engineers of MCC and its suppliers quickly to develop and implement minor and major product redesigns. For example, the first extension of the product offering was introduced within six months of launch. Two additional colours (on top of the basic ones) were introduced. The gimmick here is that a form of cubic printing is used. This technique uses not only a basic colour but adds a colour film on top of it (orange and green in this case) in a random pattern (like the spots on a cow), making each panel unique. That introduction is an important indicator of future policies. The input of Swatch, the Swiss watchmaker, in concept development is clearly present here. Within the existing product architecture of easy-to-assemble products, new options and features are introduced at a rapid pace. This adds to the fashionable character of the product: constant change and improvement.

Further ahead, the modular concept permits engineers to renew the car completely or extend the product line within short time frames. This can be achieved by changing the form of body panels and interior components, while keeping the basis of the car (the Tridion safety cell) unchanged. Through 'smart' product development, the engineers at MCC have achieved high levels of customer-perceived choice, while limiting product variation and production complexity.

Selling the concept

Smart was launched into its target European automotive market which is stagnating and where competition in existing channels is rapidly intensifying. To lend leverage to the remarkable design of the product, the marketing organisation is geared not only to promote Smart as a new car concept, but also to create new sales opportunities by using unconventional channels and sales processes.

The market winners of the car are:

- design and technology
- high levels of customer choice
- new distribution channels
- safety
- space (small size but large interior)
- environment (fuel efficiency, recyclability).

Technology relates to such features as the tip-touch gearbox, features that differentiate the product from the smaller cars of other brands that are positioned as basic and low cost. Design (form and colours) reveal the Swatch input in the concept development and give the car a trendy and different look. Customisation is actively included in the sales process by making sales channels establish a dialogue with customers and sell on a consultative rather than a 'move-the-metal' basis. In addition to the initial choices, a relationship with the customer is developed by additional customisation opportunities during the period of ownership. While customisation is not new in the automotive market, the combination of a two or three-week lead-time based on production flexibility, and direct distribution (as opposed to multilayer distribution), certainly is. VW currently has a lead-time of up to six months for some models. Space relates to the smallness of the car, allowing it to reduce congestion on roads and in parking areas. Environment, furthermore, refers to recycling and lower emission rates of the car.

After the launch of the product, the target segment of DINKies (double income, no kids) turned out to be too narrow, as the Smart proved attractive to senior citizens and also to students. The target markets were redefined to include customers that are young or young in mind and fashion conscious. Dealerships are located in highly frequented places in urbanised areas such as shopping centres on the outskirts of cities. In addition to the Smart Centres, satellites (smaller sales outlets related to a centre) are used. The function of the satellites is to increase product exposure and market penetration by adding a sub-channel. Satellites display one or two cars. Sales advisors in the satellites do not take orders; they do prepare product proposals but their main function is to attract prospective customers to the nearest Smart Centre. In Germany a satellite centre is located in a McDonald's restaurant, and in future satellites may also work through supermarkets, department stores and as shops-within-shops.

Cars are mainly built to customer orders, which the plant in Hambach receives from the Smart Centres. For the purpose of display, test rides, promotion and for 'take-away' sales, Smart Centres do have cars in stock and, if needed, the car can be customised at the centre according to the client's specification by the exchange of such components as body parts. Some further final assembling tasks, like adding special features or light final assembly, can be performed at the centres. Postponement thus plays a major role in customising the product to client's needs in the centres, but also takes place in the factory.

The single-stage sales concept allows Smart centres to procure their cars – via the sales logistics department – directly from the production plant in Hambach instead of through a dealer or import organisation. This distribution system is very different to the tiered sales structure in the traditional automotive industry, in which national sales organisations and importers add another layer between dealers and the manufacturer. Through this concept, Smart aims to minimise ordering and delivery times and to reduce cost. The dealer organisations use multimedia systems to enable clients to 'engineer' their car in the showroom and to forward orders directly to MCC headquarters. This allows production planning to be based on point-of-sale (POS) data. The centres are connected to Hambach by satellite.

SMART-ville

At the launch of the product in selected European markets, a total of DM830 million had been invested in developing and building a factory. The full capacity of the plant is 200 000 vehicles a year, or 750 a day, a volume that is targeted for the year 2000. The factory, located in Hambach, France, covers 68 hectares with 20 production buildings. A test site was built in an 18-month period. The facility is referred to as 'Smart-ville'. Suppliers and partners of MCC occupy a number of on-site buildings, and investment in factory development was shared with suppliers. MCC invested approximately DM445 million, its suppliers and partners about DM385 million. Suppliers invested a further DM300 million in machinery and facilities in the Hambach factory. Employment started with 1500 (only 650 of which are on the MCC payroll) and is expected to rise to 2200 over the next few years. MCC also invested DM700 million in the development of the car and in machinery, and DM550 million in establishing a dealer and distribution organisation. Total investment before launch reached DM2.4 billion.

Right at the start of the production, the management of MCC addressed the question of how to expand capacity in the near future. The whole concept has been developed to enable MCC to expand capacity by replicating the site, its layout and its supply structure, anywhere in the world, wherever the market may be.

Flexibility, just-in-time operation and short supply lead-times were goals for production and plant layout. According to MCC, this has resulted in a reduction of transport and logistics cost to the absolute minimum. Moreover, final assembly of the car takes just 4.5 hours, which is far less than in any other factory in the world. It is impressive to see how easily the modules and parts can be bolted to a car. Design for assembly has been taken beyond current levels. The high performance levels of the final assembly facilities could only be attained through innovative outsourcing concepts – described in the next section.

The supply chain structure

Before the supply chain is detailed, it is important to understand the product structure of MCC and how the product is divided into modules. It is impressive to see how MCC has succeeded in limiting the number of components supplied by direct (tier 1) suppliers. The modular concept, as well as technological innovations, have enabled MCC to produce a car from no more than 40 to 50 modules and parts. Table 33.1 specifies these modules and parts in terms of integrated (in-house) and non-integrated supplies.

Table 33.1 Modules and parts sourced by MCC

Integrated direct suppliers	Non-integrated suppliers				
	Ordered according to production plan		Parts and components on-the-shelf (TuF)		After sales parts, available at Smart Centre
Front module	Seats (including optional side airbags)	Rear axle	Seat belts	Brake system	Cassette-, CD-box
Body panels	Wheel system	Front axle	Locking system	Drive shaft	Cup holder
Paint and body protection	Exhaust system	Under shield	Carpet	ABS cable system	RPM revolution counter
Rear module drive-line (incl. engine)	Transmission	Cooling system	Rear light	Relays box	Audio system
Safety body cell	Headlights	Wheel arch and sill panels	Side direction indicator	Driver pedal module	Other parts – not specified
Dashboard/cockpit, including airbags	Engine		Sunshade for glass roof	Fuel tank flap	
Doors	Front window		Aerial (antenna)	Fog lights	
Cubic printing	Glass roof		Upper interior trim	Rear window	
	Roof module		SE-drive unit	10–15 other components – not specified	
	Fuel tanks		Crash management system		
	Centre console; Luggage box				

Figure 33.2 MCC basic plant layout

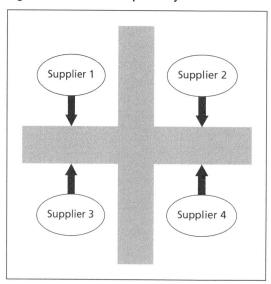

Smart is based on an integral body frame (the Tridion) to which modules are attached. Apart from the body, the car consists of several main modules:

- rear module, including the driveline
- doors
- cockpit.

Each module contains sub-modules and components. The modules are supplied in sequence for final assembly by a small number of first-tier suppliers. Seven of these are fully integrated into the final assembly site. Modules are bought by MCC only when needed for the final assembly process. For example, a complete rear module includes rear axles, transmission, suspension and engine. It is pre-assembled by a supplier, who starts assembling the module only on demand by MCC. The assembly sequence by the supplier begins 1.5 hours before the module is needed on the final assembly line. The same is true of the doors (three hours lead-time) and the dash-board system (one hour lead-time).

To ensure a smooth flow of goods within the plant, the car is moved along the workstations of the assembly line, which is laid out in the form of a cross (see Figure 33.2).

Reasons for this plant layout were to permit frequent deliveries at a large number of delivery points, while keeping transport to a minimum. Sub-sections can also work independently to avoid system disruptions in case of malfunction at one particular point along the assembly line (Figure 33.3). Furthermore, 'integrated suppliers' are able to supply their finished products directly to the final assembly line or by means of a conveyor system.

At Smart-ville, the manufacturing process starts with Magna assembling the body (Tridion) in white. This process is highly automated and standardised: Magna employs 130 robots. In fact, this is one of the very few automated process steps; operators mostly perform subsequent steps. The finished body is then passed on to the next partner in the adjoining facility. In this step Surtema (an Eisenmann

Figure 33.3 The Smart Car assembly line

subsidiary) primes and paints the body using paint tunnels for each of the two colours (black and silver/grey). The process is based on powder coating – it has been developed especially for Smart and is environmentally friendly.

After painting, the body is transferred by conveyor belt to the beginning of the assembly 'cross'. Starting at the top of the cross, VDO assembles cockpits and mounts them to the body. In the three other sections of the cross, MCC goes on assembling the car, starting with the mechanics and chassis, followed by external and internal trim assembly, inspection and testing. The rear module (including the drive train) is pre-assembled by Krupp Hoesch and undergoes several additional assembly tasks by MCC workers on a small island adjacent to the cross. Following assembly, the rear module is brought to the line on a telescopic carrier that raises it to shoulder height, enabling operators to guide it into the car.

During the assembly process, modules and components are delivered line-side (within 10 metres of the workstation) on a just-in-time basis. For example, complete front-end and rear-end modules are delivered by Bosch and Krupp respectively. Dynamit Nobel delivers the plastic outer body panels moulded on site. The door panels are delivered to Magna Door Systems, who pre-assemble the doors before delivering them line-side. The seven 'integrated' suppliers are responsible for the supply of 70–80 per cent of the volume and 30–40 per cent of the value of the finished product. In addition, 16 non-integrated suppliers deliver sub-modules and parts to both MCC and the integrated suppliers. These non-integrated suppliers add about another 20 per cent of the volume to the car. Their supplies include seats, wheels, windows, etc. and are delivered to the relevant docking station of the assembly line, at a maximum distance of 10 metres. The remaining 10 per cent of the volume consist of standard and small parts not linked to a particular module, which are stored in an on-site warehouse, operated by a third party.

MCC has selected suppliers to integrate at the site and suppliers that could supply from a distant location by a straightforward process. Logistics management at MCC made a calculation based on the frequency at which a module was used and its size. The outcome of this exercise showed the volume of the various flows of components. Apart from special cases in which the characteristics of the manufacturing process did not allow on-site assembly (as with engines), the components causing the largest transport flows were integrated in the premises of MCC. Table 33.2 lists the integrated and non-integrated suppliers of MCC.

Table 33.2 Selection of MCC suppliers

Integrated module suppliers

1	Bosch	Front module and headlights
2	Dynamit Nobel	Synthetic body panels/wheel arch and sill panels
3	Surtema	Paint and surface protection
4	Cubic	Cubic printing
5	Krupp Hoesch	Rear module (rear-wheel suspension, integration of engine, etc.)
6	Magna/Magna Doors System	Safety body cell/doors
7	VDO	Dashboard/cockpit, battery and wiring harnesses

Non-integrated main suppliers

1	Behr	Cooling system
2	Bertrand Faure	Seats
3	Continental	Tyres
4	Eberspächer	Exhaust system
5	Getrag	Transmission
6	Magneti Marelli	Dynamo/starter/relays
7	DaimlerChrysler	Engine/front and rear axles/drive shaft
8	Splintex	Windows and glass roof
9	Meritor	Roof-module, sunshade for glass roof
10	Bosch	Control/stability system
11	Solvay	Fuel tanks
12	Stankiewicz	Carpet
13	Simoldes	Centre console and luggage boxes
14	Rieter	Undershield
15	Johnson Controls Interiors	Upper interior trim
16	Lemförder	SE-drive unit
(17*)	Dynamit Nobel	Crash management system
(18*)	Bosch	Headlights/brake systems

'TuF' suppliers = non-integrated suppliers of off-the-shelf products

10 (16*)	Various suppliers	Ranging from, among others, heater-aircon systems, driver pedal systems and side airbags, to fog lights

Suppliers marked with * supply in multiple supply chain setting; they perform both as integrated and as non-integrated suppliers.

The system also differs from traditional supply chains with respect to the activities that are outsourced. Even activities traditionally considered core activities of the OEM (original equipment manufacturer), such as the pressing of body parts and painting, and even the coordination of internal logistics, are no longer performed by MCC. Not only do suppliers closely participate in the final assembly of the car, they are also deeply involved in the development and planning of the product. What can be said about the outsourcing of components and modules manufacturing is equally true of supporting services. The whole information system supporting the processes of MCC in manufacturing, logistics and distribution is outsourced to a third-party service provider, who owns and exploits the hardware and the software, as a facility-management arrangement. Panopa controls lorry traffic on site, which is important because 100 lorry deliveries will be made during each shift once full capacity is reached. TNT logistics manages a spare-part facility and Rhenus operates a storage facility for small standard components and parts. These parts are replenished to the line by a *kanban* pull system, operated by Rhenus. MTL, finally, ships finished cars to the dealers. Production output is shipped instantly and directly to the dealers without intermediate hold-ups or inventory layers.

Supplier relations

The plant in Hambach was in every sense a greenfield. The car was novel, supplier relations had to be built up, the plant was completely new, and even the organisation and its staff had been built from scratch. Therefore, the building of supplier relations was not saddled with history. Following the first crude drawings of the car and its modules, several suppliers were invited to send in competitive bids for product concepts. The concept competition (Konzept-Wettbewerb) resulted in proposals of suppliers with respect to, among other things: the modules in terms of functions, materials, layout, design, etc.; suggested production technologies, processes and location, as well as logistic systems; and target cost.

In developing the supply chain, a detailed supply chain map was developed including descriptions of processes and sub-processes involved, and establishing which company would be solely, partially or informally responsible for each of the 140 assembly activities in the process. To develop the modules, project teams consisting of MCC and selected suppliers worked together and reported to an MCC team coach. The supplier involvement in design was structured within the general product architecture specified by MCC.

Contracts with suppliers are intended to last the entire life cycle of the product, and are based upon single-sourced modules. In line with that principle, the contract with only one supplier has so far been terminated because it could not meet quality standards over a period of time.

The initial rationale for involving suppliers was in fact a financial one. At the time the project was proposed to the Daimler board, the automotive industry had reached the stage of saturation and a (temporarily) stagnating demand, and many automotive companies were busy restructuring their programmes. The go-ahead for the project was based on the relatively low investment costs for Daimler, given the large share contributed by suppliers.

To facilitate communication and the exchange of ideas among staff and partners, a central area of the factory is designed as a meeting room. Its function as 'marketplace' is reinforced by its use for open discussion of problems and for quality management and quality improvement meetings. Furthermore, standardised performance measures for each sub-section of the process are displayed electronically at the 'marketplace', for everyone to see. Measures include assembly line stoppage times, delivery performance, product reclamation and scrap, productivity targets and trends, as well as qualifications of teams/sections along the line. The open architecture of the factory makes quality problems and line-stops clearly visible to clerical employees as well as to assembly workers. Cars that need to be fixed because of quality problems or missing components are parked at the 'marketplace'.

Questions

Despite the innovative achievements, MCC management was facing a number of immediate and longer-term issues, centring on how to manage and control the supply chain.

1   *Why should MCC assemble cars itself when suppliers are already integrated on the site? VW, for example, at its truck plant in Latin America, involves suppliers in assembly, thus further lowering the financial commitment of the OEM. In line with the question whether car makers should assemble cars at all, or should leave this to suppliers, an interesting topic is how to assure a lead over suppliers when these perform most of the value-adding activities and how to maintain an integrated environment. One might reason that suppliers are becoming too 'smart' and might (in a consortium or stand-alone) bypass MCC and gain the lead over the supply chain. The Lear Corporation, for example, is a consortium of suppliers that used to supply car-interior parts to manufacturers and is now beginning to supply entire car interiors and so is becoming increasingly dominant in relations with manufacturers.*

2   *Another problem was how to control and assure performance in the supply chain, not on the basis of ownership but through cooperation with suppliers. MCC is heavily focused on integrating the flow of information between players and levels in the chain, but how should the performance of partners be measured and assured?*

3   *The order to delivery lead-time is generally faster than other manufacturers. However, visiting the Smart user club at **www.thesmartclub.co.uk** revealed such problems as:*

> *'Just picked up my new Smart Pash tonight. Been dead excited all day. However, there were a few things not quite right when I got to Smart Milton Keynes (MK Smart):*

> – *Colour was wrong. I ordered a blue one. Def ordered blue. Car is silver, but I think I prefer the silver one now!!!!*
> – *No CD multi-changer fitted, as ordered. More gutted about this really, I have no tapes at all, so the weekend driving will be listening to crappy radio! MK Smart say they will get me in early next week to have this fitted.*
> – *No velour mats as ordered. They say they had none. Fair point, mats are not essential (unlike CD player!), but they will supply my mats when they are in.*

> > *'All in all, I was a little disappointed, but the total handover was very well explained by Giles, and they were very apologetic about the missing bits and bobs.*
> > *'I wanted to specify it with Boomerang Red seats, but was told that this would be a special order taking up to 12 weeks (!!) as there is a run on Smarts at the moment. So I accepted a car they already had in stock with Blue seats, but had all the clock/rev counter/speedo/controls with red trims ... and I collected it three weeks later ...'*

Taking into account that (a) it is possible to have order-specific modules such as dashboards produced at two hours' notice, and (b) the final assembly process takes less than five hours, why is a response time of two to three weeks such a challenge for MCC?

4 *The modular product concept of MCC permits customisation of the product in the dealer channel through logistical postponement. However, at present the final assembly is done at the plant in Hambach. What could be the rationale behind that decision?*

Supplying fast fashion[13]

Garment retailing has changed. No longer is there a standard look that all retailers adhere to for a whole season. Fashion is fast, complex and furious. Different trends overlap and fashion ideas that are not even on a store's radar screen can become 'must haves' within six months. Many retail businesses with their own brands, such as H&M and Zara, sell up-to-the-minute fashionability at low prices in stores that are clearly focused on one particular market. In the world of fast fashion, catwalk designs speed their way into high street stores at prices anyone can afford. The quality of the garment means that it may only last one season, but fast fashion customers don't want yesterday's trends. As *Newsweek* puts it, '. . . *being a "quicker picker-upper" is what made fashion retailers H&M and Zara successful. [They] thrive by practising the new science of "fast fashion", compressing product development cycles as much as six times.'* But the retail operations that customers see are only the end part of the supply chains that feeds them. And these have also changed.

At its simplest level, the fast fashion supply chain has four stages. First, the garments are designed, after which they are manufactured, they are then distributed to the retail outlets where they are displayed and sold in retail operations designed to reflect the business's brand values. In this short case study, we examine two fast fashion operations, Hennes and Mauritz (known as H&M) and Zara, together with United Colours of Benetton (UCB), a similar chain, but with a different market positioning.

United Colours of Benetton. Almost 50 years ago Luciano Benetton took the world of fashion by storm by selling the bright, casual sweaters designed by his sister across Europe (and later the rest of the world), promoted by controversial advertising. By 2005, the Benetton Group was present in 120 countries throughout the world. Selling casual garments, mainly under its United Colours of Benetton (UCB) and its more fashion-oriented Sisley brands, it produces 110 million garments a year, over 90 per cent of them in Europe. Its retail network of over 5,000 stores produces revenue of around €2 billion. Benetton products are seen as less 'high fashion' but of higher quality and durability, and with higher prices, than H&M and Zara.

H&M. Established in Sweden in 1947, H&M now sell clothes and cosmetics in over 1,000 stores in 20 countries

Source: KevinFoy/Alamy Images

around the world. The business concept is 'fashion and quality at the best price'. With more than 40,000 employees, and revenues of around SEK 60,000 million, its biggest market is Germany, followed by Sweden and the UK. H&M are seen by many as the originator of the fast fashion concept. Certainly they have years of experience at driving down the price of up-to-the-minute fashions. *'We ensure the best price,'* they say, *'by having few middlemen, buying large volumes, having extensive experience of the clothing industry, having a great knowledge of which goods should be bought from which markets, having efficient distribution systems, and being cost-conscious at every stage.'*

Zara. The first store opened almost by accident in 1975 when Amancio Ortega Gaona, a women's pyjama manufacturer, was left with a large cancelled order. The shop he opened was intended only as an outlet for cancelled orders. Now, Inditex, the holding group that includes the Zara brand, has over 1,300 stores in 39 countries with sales of over €3 billion. The Zara brand accounts for over 75 per cent of the group's total retail sales, and is still based in north-west Spain. By 2003 it had become the world's fastest growing volume garment retailer. The Inditex group also has several other branded chains including Pull and Bear, and Massimo Dutti. In total it employs almost 40,000 people in a business that is known for a high degree of vertical integration compared with most fast fashion companies. The company believes that it is their integration along the supply chain that allows them to respond to customer demand fast and flexibly while keeping stock to a minimum.

Design

All three businesses emphasise the importance of design in this market. Although not *haute couture*, capturing design trends is vital to success. Even the boundary between high and fast fashion is starting to blur. In 2004, H&M recruited high fashion designer Karl Lagerfeld, previous noted for his work with more exclusive brands. For H&M his designs were priced for value rather than exclusivity. *'Why do I work for H&M? Because I believe in inexpensive clothes, not 'cheap' clothes,'* said Lagerfeld. Yet most of H&M's products come from over 100 designers in Stockholm who work with a team of 50 pattern designers, around 100 buyers and a number of budget controllers. The department's task is to find the optimum balance between the three components comprising H&M's business concept – fashion, price and quality. Buying volumes and delivery dates are then decided.

Zara's design functions are organised in a different way to most similar companies. Conventionally, the design input comes from three *separate* functions: the designers themselves, market specialists, and buyers who place orders on to suppliers. At Zara the design stage is split into three product areas: women's, men's and children's garments. In each area, designers, market specialists and buyers are co-located in design halls that also contain small workshops for trying out prototype designs. The market specialists in all three design halls are in regular contact with Zara retail stores, discussing customer reaction to new designs. In this way, the retail stores are not the end of the whole supply chain but the beginning of the design stage of the chain. Zara's around 300 designers, whose average age is 26, produce approximately 40,000 items per year of which about 10,000 go into production.

Benetton also has around 300 designers, who not only design for all their brands, but also are engaged in researching new materials and clothing concepts. Since 2000, the company has moved to standardise their range globally. At one time more than 20 per cent of its ranges were customised to the specific needs of each country, now only between 5 and 10 per cent of garments are customised. This reduced the number of individual designs offered globally by over 30 per cent, strengthening the global brand image and reducing production costs.

Both H&M and Zara have moved away from the traditional industry practice of offering two 'collections' a year, for Spring/Summer and Autumn/Winter. Their 'seasonless cycle' involves the continual introduction of new products on a rolling basis throughout the year. This allows designers to learn from customers' reactions to their new products and incorporate them quickly into more new products. The most extreme version of this idea is practiced by Zara. A garment will be designed; a batch manufactured and 'pulsed' through the supply chain. Often the design is never repeated, it may be modified and another batch produced, but there are no 'continuing' designs as such. Even Benetton, have increased the proportion of what they call 'flash' collections, small collections that are put into its stores during the season.

Manufacturing

At one time Benetton focused its production on its Italian plants. Then it significantly increased its production outside Italy to take advantage of lower labour costs. Non-Italian operations include factories in North Africa, Eastern Europe and Asia. Yet each location operates in a very similar manner. A central, Benetton owned, operation performs some manufacturing operations (especially those requiring expensive technology) and coordinates the more labour intensive production activities that are performed by a network of smaller contractors (often owned and managed by ex-Benetton employees). These contractors may in turn sub-contract some of their activities. The company's central facility in Italy allocates production to each of the non-Italian networks, deciding what and how much each is to produce. There is some specialisation, for example, jackets are made in Eastern Europe while T-shirts are made in Spain. Benetton also has a controlling share in its main supplier of raw materials, to ensure fast supply to its factories. Benetton are also known for the practice of dying garments after assembly rather than using died thread or fabric. This postpones decisions about colours until late in the supply process so that there is a greater chance of producing what is needed by the market.

H&M does not have any factories of its own, but instead works with around 750 suppliers. Around half of production takes place in Europe and the rest mainly in Asia. It has 21 production offices around the world that between them are responsible for coordinating the suppliers who produce over half a billion items a year for H&M. The relationship between production offices and suppliers is vital, because it allows fabrics to be bought in early. The actual dyeing and cutting of the garments can then be decided at a later stage in the production The later an order can be placed on suppliers, the less the risk of buying the wrong thing. Average supply lead times vary from three weeks up to six months, depending on the nature of the goods. *'The most important thing,'* they say, *'is to find the optimal time to order each item. Short lead times are not always best. For some high-volume fashion basics, it is to our advantage to place orders far in advance. Trendier garments require considerably shorter lead times.'*

Zara's lead times are said to be the fastest in the industry, with a 'catwalk to rack' time as little as 15 days. According to one analyst, this is because they *'owned most of the manufacturing capability used to make their products, which they use as a means of exciting and stimulating customer demand.'* About half of Zara's products are produced in its network of 20 Spanish factories, which, like at Benetton, tend to concentrate on the more capital intensive operations such as cutting and dyeing. Sub-contractors are used for most labour intensive operations like sewing. Zara buy around 40 per cent of their fabric from its own wholly-owned subsidiary, most of which is in undyed form for dyeing after assembly. Most Zara factories and their sub-contractors work on a single shift system to retain some volume flexibility.

Distribution

Both Benetton and Zara have invested in highly automated warehouses, close to their main production centres that store, pack and assemble individual orders for their retail networks. These automated warehouses represent a major investment for both companies. In 2001, Zara caused some press comment by announcing that it would open a second automated warehouse even though, by its own calculations, it was only using about half its existing warehouse capacity. More recently, Benetton caused some controversy by announcing that it was exploring the use of RFID tags to track its garments.

At H&M, while the stock management is primarily handled internally, physical distribution is subcontracted. A large part of the flow of goods is routed from production site to the retail country via H&M's transit terminal in Hamburg. Upon arrival the goods are inspected and allocated to the stores or to the centralised store stock room. The centralised store stock room, within H&M referred to as 'Call-Off Warehouse' replenishes stores on item level according to what is selling.

Retail

All H&M stores (average size 1,300 square metres) are owned and solely run by H&M. The aim is to *'create a comfortable and inspiring atmosphere in the store that makes it simple for customers to find what they want and to feel at home'*. This is similar to Zara stores, although they tend to be smaller (average size 800 square metres). Perhaps the most remarkable characteristic of Zara stores is that garments rarely stay in the store for longer than two weeks. Because product designs are often not repeated and are produced in relatively small batches, the range of garments displayed in the store can change radically every two or three week. This encourages customers both to avoid delaying a purchase and to revisit the store frequently.

Since 2000 Benetton has been reshaping its retail operations. At one time the vast majority of Benetton retail outlets were small shops run by third parties. Now these small stores have been joined by several, Benetton owned and operated, larger stores (average size 1,500 to 3,000 square metres). These mega-stores can display the whole range of Benetton products and reinforce the Benetton shopping experience.

QUESTION

Compare and contrast the approaches taken by H&M, Benetton and Zara to managing their supply chain.

Case Example 6.6   Northwards Housing

Social housing is provided by local authorities (councils) and not-for-profit organisations such as housing associations and is allocated on the basis of need to people at risk, the homeless or those on low incomes. Northwards Housing is a not-for-profit company created by Manchester City Council, a large metropolitan council in the north-west of England, to manage some of the council's properties. The company provides estate management services, caretaking services, repairs and maintenance services and property improvements to their tenants. Robin Lawler, Northward's chief executive, explained:

Source: Northwards Housing

Our area covers the north part of Manchester including some quite tough areas with higher than average unemployment. Our vision is to continue to improve north Manchester by delivering an innovative housing service which involves all customers and stakeholders. Our objectives are to provide warm, safe and affordable homes for all our tenants through advice, support and a multi-million pound investment programme, which creates jobs for local people and provides excellent value for money. I believe by working with tenants and other agencies and partners we will not only contribute to the regeneration of north Manchester, but also develop successful communities and help to reduce crime, fear of crime and anti-social behaviour.

We work closely with the private contractors who do the repairs and maintenance on our properties. We are now moving to a more partnering approach with long-term relationships with a small number of contractors to help us design and deliver our major improvements programme. With these partners we will agree what we want to achieve and together agree a process between us; so it's not a case of us giving them a specification and then standing over them while they do it. We also review the work after each phase and we ask the people who have been on the receiving end how satisfied were they, how good were the contractors, how good was the service, and try and learn from that. It all seems to work well. Our levels of satisfaction are about 9.8 out of 10 for repairs.

With our contractors we go for a 'no surprises approach'. We give them lists of properties and information about layout etc. then also tell them what to expect in terms of the people who live there and any special requirements they have. Then the contractor sends in their people to design the heating system, bathroom or whatever and they come back to talk to us if there is an issue or a problem. We leave them to do a lot of the liaising with the client. They are much more customer focused than they have been in the past when you might have a grumpy builder come in and rip out the kitchen and put one in around you without considering you and your needs.

This is all quite a different way of working for us and it's taken us some time to get our heads around it. But it's a much better arrangement for everyone involved than the more traditional adversarial, single contract for each job approach. It has also been cheaper; we have made major efficiency savings so we can reinvest the savings to do other things even better. For example if we are changing the kitchen and bathroom (which we usually do together) in a retirement flat we will also redecorate the whole flat while we are there. It's been a bit of a challenge for some of our staff where there was a feeling that you just can't trust a contractor, but we have found that contractors actually seem to enjoy working like this, taking responsibility, and then doing a better job!

In terms of our suppliers, we now work with about six other social housing organisations and have created a procurement consortium, where we pool our experience, share best practice and work together to get a better rate from our suppliers.

We also like to look at things in a much more holistic way, for example we need to do our bit but the police also need to get their bit right, and the council need to do their bit, clean the streets and maintain the play areas for example. We now have structured meetings with an agreed action plan to align all our activities and resources. There are also many informal meetings and phone calls to sort things out. We also have task team meetings when we meet with the police, council officers and others and we might decide to concentrate on a small area, a neighbourhood, identify the issues and the hot spots and decide how, together, we will deal with them. So for example, when we decide to do a blitz in an area we might encourage or help residents tidy up their gardens and make sure their properties are in good condition. The police deal with people with warrants against them for example, and the council will go in and remove untaxed cars and clear up the spare land.

We also work alongside council officers and police community support officers and private sector housing colleagues to consult residents and faith groups about what they see as the priorities for their community. We try to find out what the real problems are – often things like drug dealing, off road biking and rubbish dumping. We also ask them what they would like to see done with bits of spare land etc. and then involve them with the design of things. This co-ordinated approach has a huge impact.

We have also deployed different resources like neighbourhood wardens to go into hot spot areas. It's not just about chasing kids off one street corner to the next, but it's about creating youth engagement projects to give young people worthwhile things to do. The wardens run model car racing, football competitions and so on. We've run a Food and Dance Festival; we've paid for a music project to be done. We have even created junior wardens with all the primary schools who help with picking up litter, making sure that the lights aren't left on, or the taps aren't running in the toilets. We hope this kind of social responsibility spills over into the community as well.

We also work with social services when issues arise. Our contractors sometimes come across cases of domestic abuse and the breakdown of families, so we have developed some processes alongside the police and social services so when our contractors go in and spot problems, they know what to do.

In the past we used to have some big problems in some areas with anti-social behaviour with gangs of people roaming round smashing up cars and houses and you might have the police saying it's a housing problem and the housing saying it's a council problem etc. Now we are all joined up. Now it's a shared problem and we get together to work out what are the real issues and deal with them. It's all about everyone having the right to live safely in an area, looking after themselves, their homes and kids so they can have a peaceful life.

RAC Motoring Services

Case date
2000   Stuart Chambers

'I think that we all now fully understand the need for some fairly radical reorganisation of the way we plan and operate a rescue service, but I'm not convinced that we yet fully appreciate just how difficult this is going to be! The changes to our business environment in the last few years have been quite dramatic, and if we are to remain profitable we must now complete our negotiations with the unions in order to implement the new systems we have devised. Lex bought the RAC on the basis of its strong brand, large customer base and good profitability. However, if we don't get this work completed quickly, our service levels will continue to be worse than some leading competitors, and could even fall. We will certainly lose market share, and our costs will rise inexorably. At the moment, the only big winners seem to be the contractors who provide capacity during the night and when we are overloaded. And whilst our own patrol staff are earning more and more, their productivity is continuing to decline. We have no choice: we must solve this one, or we will be in serious trouble.'

Martin Connor, the Director of Operations, was addressing the monthly meeting of the operations team, just prior to the commencement of a series of negotiations with representatives of the Transport and General Workers Union (TGWU), which was the recognised union for the majority of the manual employees.

The RAC

RAC Motoring Services had been established in the vehicle breakdown and recovery industry for over 100 years. It had its own branded patrol force which was deployed to rescue and fix customers vehicles at the roadside. The RAC was perceived to offer a high-quality service at a relatively high price. However, its image had sometimes been seen as somewhat old-fashioned. Its brand was very well established and trusted, but it was the number two in terms of customer awareness behind the AA (Automobile Association). For all of their long histories, until very recently both these organisations were owned by a specific group of their members, and were therefore not required to produce profits for external shareholders. Some commentators believed that this type of mutuality inevitably led to a sense of complacency, where market share was the most important measure of success. Underlying this image, however, the RAC had continued to invest in state-of-the-art technologies to efficiently receive members' calls and to dispatch rescue patrols. It had also constructed eye-catching control centres at highly visible points on the motorway systems, signalling its presence as a modern service provider.

In order to overcome its slightly dated image, in 1997 the RAC had rebranded and changed its corporate colours, the aim being to project a more modern and dynamic image to appeal to younger market segments. This was primarily done to address the continuing erosion of market share, but the main reason for its declining customer base had been the increasing level of competition in the market. For many years the RAC and AA had dominated the market, but recent new players such as Green Flag had entered by offering a cheaper product using third-party contractors. This introduced price competition and redefined customer service expectation. Green Flag advertised aggressively that it would reach all customers within 35 minutes, and if it did not, then it would refund £10. This led to Green Flag rapidly gaining market share at the expense of the AA and RAC.

In 1999 both the RAC and the AA gave up their mutuality when they were taken over by a large companies. The AA was acquired by Centrica, a utility services company, and the RAC by Lex plc, which included vehicle servicing businesses, vehicle leasing and the British School of Motoring. This brought a more commercial focus to both organisations. The RAC was determined not only to arrest the decline in customer numbers, but also to rapidly increase it. It could not do this by acquisition, and therefore the only option was to invest so that it could lead the market in terms of service quality.

A recent independent survey, carried out by J D Power, ranked the RAC second behind the AA in terms of customer satisfaction. The AA was ahead in two key areas: the quality of its call-taking (when customers phone the organisation to request roadside assistance) and the efficiency of its dispatch system (getting patrols to the customer quickly). The roadside services provided by patrols from both organisations were similar. The AA's more advanced call-taking and dispatch system resulted in quicker response times and better customer management during the period that customers were waiting for service. Therefore, for the RAC to grow its market share, it definitely needed to improve its call-taking and dispatch processes. It should be noted, however, that a leading 'new' competitor had scored consistently low in the J D Power survey for all aspects of its service, but continued to compete on the basis of lower annual membership charges.

Customers were getting more demanding too. Expectations of service quality are continuously rising, and motorists who have broken down invariably feel stressed and anxious. The quality of every interaction between the RAC and its members will be of concern. Thus customers will perceive waiting time as critical, and the reliability of arrival time of the patrol will be under scrutiny. Martin Connor was only too aware of the importance of reliability, as failure to meet lead-time promises had a major effect on customer satisfaction levels, and these were measured regularly by independent market researchers.

The patrols

By 1999, the RAC was employing about 1350 patrols, and most of these had followed an earlier career as mechanics, undertaking garage servicing of vehicles. In many ways these were considered to be the elite of the mechanics trade, since they were capable, through experience and further training, of servicing a very wide range of vehicles and associated faults, usually in the presence of the distressed customer and in harsh roadside conditions. These skills were well rewarded by good earnings, including overtime payments, well above those of the garage trade. However, the average age of the patrols was becoming fairly high, and many were beginning to contemplate retirement. Surprisingly, patrol turnover was remarkably low, at around three per cent,

Patrols worked on rotating patterns of shifts referred to as 'Earlies' (7:00 to 15:00), 'Mids' (11:00 to 19:00) and 'Lates' (15:00 to 23:00). However, very few patrols (around five per cent) were scheduled for the Mids, because demand for roadside assistance tended to be lower through the middle of the day, certainly on weekdays. Together, the normal patrols in any cell evenly covered all seven days of a week, with every patrol working a third of the days on Earlies, a third on Lates, and a third taking a break period. Each of the patrols was issued with its own fully equipped rescue vehicle, which was only needed during working hours. When not required, this vehicle would usually be parked outside home, ready for the next use. Although this resulted in low utilisation of this very expensive asset, this had been found to be the best way of ensuring that the equipment was kept in a good condition ready for use. It also ensured that the patrol could continue to work on a broken-down vehicle even beyond the end of its shift, without worrying about the delay in handing over to another patrol. It also allowed the patrol to be on 'standby', awaiting a request to attend a motorist outside the normal shift time. This provided the patrol an opportunity for overtime earnings, whilst giving the RAC extra capacity to call on at off-peak times.

Managing the patrols

The patrols were organised into geographic 'cells'. These varied in size from about 8 to 15 patrols, covering an area that allowed a patrol to travel to reach a motorist within about 20 minutes. Under average conditions, this would allow a patrol to attend about one job per hour: say 20 minutes travel, 20 minutes to undertake the repair and 20 minutes average delay awaiting the next call-out. During busy periods the average waiting time would become much lower. The office-based dispatching operations were conducted on the basis of these cells; motorists breaking down within a particular cell were normally serviced by a patrol from that cell.

About 50 service managers were each responsible for teams of up to 28 patrols covering two or three cells. Their job was to ensure that service standards were achieved in their areas, within target productivity levels. However, an activity survey in 1998 indicated that they generally attempted to achieve this by undertaking a large number of odd jobs to ensure that their patrols were kept on the road. For example, they would obtain and deliver replacement uniforms and consumables to individual patrols. It was becoming very apparent that, in effect, they were spending their time circumventing or supplementing poor processes, rather than getting involved with the detailed operations management of their teams.

Use of contractors

There was extensive use of private contractors during weekends and at night-time. Sometimes they would even be used to supplement capacity during the day if unexpectedly high demand occurred. Whilst these were responsible for the same activities as patrols, they did not carry the full RAC branding, and were often found to lack the full capabilities of the patrols. Market research indicated that members were generally less satisfied with the service provided by such contractors, but it had been necessary to use them to provide capacity at times when it was uneconomical to maintain a full coverage of RAC patrols. The cost of contractors was high (averaging £36 per job) and rising, and there was considerable concern that the amount of work put out to contract was increasing, at the same time that the productivity of the patrols was actually falling.

The proportion of jobs covered by patrols was measured every month; the Patrol Attendance Rate (PAR) was averaging 80 per cent in 1999. It had been calculated that a one per cent fall in PAR would cost about £1 million per year in contractor fees. Therefore, in order to generally minimise the use of contractors, patrols had always been offered incentives to do some of the jobs at off-peak times. The PAR was often low at times when the patrols took holidays, for example many were on leave at the end of the holiday year (March), and many patrols wanted to take their holiday in August to be with their families. The PAR reached a record low of 77 per cent in August 1998.

Overtime and standby

The patrols were contracted to work shift rosters, as described earlier, over a standard 40-hour week. In general, when demand was expected to be sufficiently high, they were offered overtime work or per job payments known as 'standby'. Overtime was paid at time-and-a-half rates (approximately £10 per hour) with double time on Sundays (approximately £14 per hour). On this basis, there was really no incentive to work fast and productively, since the patrols would be paid even whilst they waited for further instructions.

Patrols could also choose to be on standby. For this to apply, they had to 'log on' to the communications system in their vehicle, awaiting jobs to be issued to them. For every job completed they would be paid a flat fee of £6. For simple jobs (starting problems, flat battery, etc.) a patrol in a busy area could complete up to four jobs in an hour. Thus their earning potential could be very high, but they retained the right to 'log off' at will. Experience indicated that this would often happen if a difficult job was offered, which the patrol knew would take a long time. If none of the patrols in a cell would accept that job, it would then be passed to a contractor.

In 1999, only about 50–55 per cent of jobs were done within the duty roster. The remainder was covered by overtime, standby and contractors. A particular problem that arose from this system was that of inconsistent service level. The operation ran with the risk that off-peak but unexpectedly busy periods could not be adequately covered by patrols; the alternative use of contractors would often impact customer perceived service quality. Analysis of the customer feedback forms, filled in by motorists after receiving assistance, indicated a strong negative correlation between their overall satisfaction level (known as the Customer Satisfaction Index, or CSI) and the time they had waited for the patrol to arrive (known as the Average Time of Arrival, or ATA). Moreover, there was a significant seasonality in the CSI scores, with below-average levels in the winter months for two years running.

The net result was that the productivity levels achieved by the RAC patrols had been falling for five years. During this period new competitors, such as Green Flag, did not carry the cost of directly employed patrols and their associated vehicles and equipment. They simply contracted all work to third parties.

Clearly this situation could not be allowed to continue! Martin and his team had to rethink how the existing numbers of patrols, and their area service managers, could be reorganised to increase productivity and PAR. For the RAC to satisfy the changing demands of its customers and its employees, things would have to change! No longer could the organisation continue to place more and more work in the hands of contractors: it was much too costly and was certainly affecting customer satisfaction. Martin knew that there would be resistance to almost any proposed change. After all, many of the patrols were of an age where their families had left home so their living expenses were falling, and therefore they were seeking more social hours and a generally easier working schedule.

Demand patterns

The annual number of breakdowns attended by the patrols peaked in the mid-1990s at around 2.9 million, but had then fallen steadily to about 2.4 million in 1999, despite an increase in membership. This fall was attributed to several underlying factors. Firstly, the most obvious reason was that new cars had become significantly more reliable! Secondly, because of strict testing requirements, many older and more unreliable vehicles were being scrapped earlier, or were being used less, as families became multiple car owners. Thirdly, the RAC had been proactive in encouraging its members to prevent common failures. For example, a very common task for patrols involved starting cars with flat batteries. Where one was found to be old and in poor condition, the member was now required to replace it immediately, with a clear understanding that failure to do so would disqualify them from receiving this service again. This change was known to account for a reduction of approximately 150 000 incidents of this type. A second change was the introduction of the 'Fair Call Policy' which entitled a member to a maximum of six free call-outs per year; the seventh and subsequent ones would become chargeable. About three per cent of customers had created about 20 per cent of call-outs, so this policy helped to contain demand, freeing capacity and responsiveness for the less-frequent users. Despite the significant reduction in the number of breakdowns, the number of patrols was maintained at around 1350. It was calculated that even with the reducing volume of demand, the RAC would need around 2000 patrols to cope with demand without the use of contractors and overtime working. Clearly, a 50 per cent increase in numbers employed would be impracticable and too costly in terms of both capital and revenue.

Figure 20.1 RAC national total annual service breakdowns (by month)

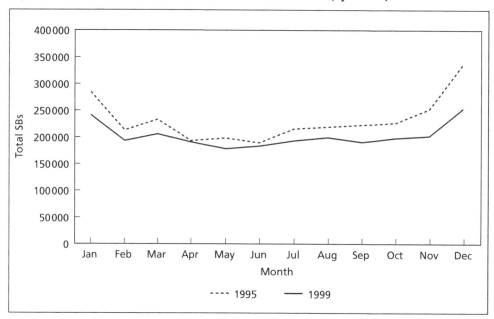

There was a significant seasonality in breakdowns, as shown in Figure 20.1. There are more call-outs in the winter, much of which can be explained by the weather. For example, electrical faults occur more frequently because extra loads are placed on the system by the greater use of lights, which are also used more of the time, providing more opportunities for failure to be noticed. Starter motors and alternators are subject to more load, and electrical systems can be affected by dampness and water ingress. In the summer, a greater proportion of the motoring population will be abroad on holiday, reducing demand on the motoring rescue services. However, to an extent offsetting this effect, a proportion of motorists take their cars on unusually long journeys on their summer holidays, sometimes heavily loaded and without adequate servicing, resulting in breakdowns such as overheating.

There were 'normal' weekly and daily patterns of service breakdown (referred to as SB) volumes that varied relatively predictably throughout the year, but this could be greatly distorted by unusually severe weather conditions. These demand patterns had gradually changed during the latter half of the 1990s as a result of gradual social, behavioral and economic changes. For example, the working population of the UK increased, leading to more home-to-work travel by car at peak times. Many organisations, ranging from manufacturers to financial services' call-centres had introduced new working patterns such as 'continental shifts', which required employees to cover operations for up to 168 hours a week. Weekend and evening shopping became much more popular, with some supermarkets staying open overnight. Fast food outlets, leisure facilities, and even universities began operating longer hours. These types of changes gradually led to a more spread-out pattern of car travel both for worker and consumers, and had noticeably reduced the weekday morning peaks SB levels. Figure 20.2 shows typical weekly patterns of demand in 1995 and 1999, Figure 20.3 shows the daily SB patterns for Saturdays, and Figure 20.4 shows the corresponding SB pattern for Mondays.

Figure 20.2 RAC total annual service breakdowns (by day of week)

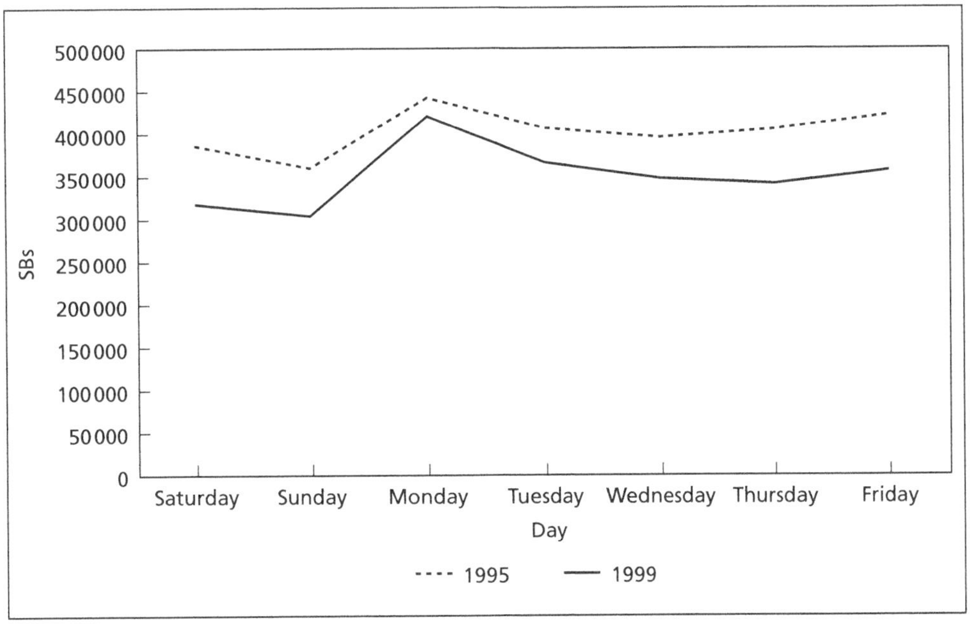

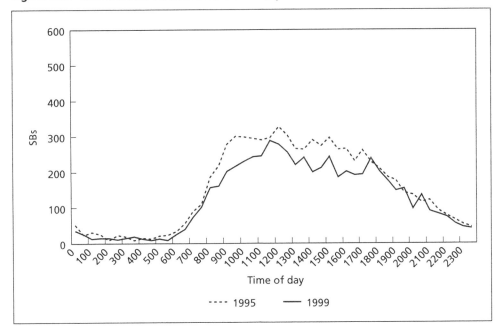

Figure 20.3 RAC national service breakdowns (by half hour for average Saturdays)

Figure 20.4   RAC national service breakdowns (by half hour for average Mondays)

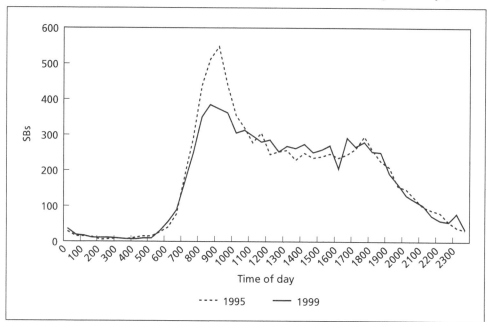

Questions

1   *Evaluate the competitive position of RAC Motoring Services in terms of its operations-based strengths or weaknesses.*

2   *What are the advantages and disadvantages of the current cell-focused service management structure? What alternatives might give better results in terms of increasing quality and productivity?*

3   *How could the employment contracts, payment systems and working practices be redesigned to help to increase the patrol productivity, to increase PAR and to reduce waiting times? What resistance is likely to be faced, and how should this best be countered?*

4   *What are your overall recommendations for an implementation plan?*

Case Exercise   The Squire Hotel Group

The Squire Hotel Group (SHG) runs a chain of 20 hotels, with between 40 and 120 bedrooms, in locations that include Oxford, Warwick and Southport. SHG sees itself in the three-star market, with hotels that have their own personality and style, providing high-quality food and service at an affordable price. The majority of mid-week guests are commercial clients. The normal mid-week occupancy rate is about 80 per cent. Weekend occupancy is about 30 per cent, comprising mainly weekend-break packages. The company does not have any major expansion plans but is trying to strengthen its existing market position.

Squire's managing director, Justin Palmer, believes that it has a high degree of customer loyalty in the commercial sector. He explains:

> The hotel managers are expected to integrate with their local community through Chambers of Commerce and Round Tables, primarily to gain visibility but also to demonstrate a local and caring attitude. The image they try to create is a good-quality, small and friendly hotel that local business can rely upon for their visitors. The hotel managers are expected to work hard to develop personal relationships with local firms and may also try to promote other hotels in the chain for any 'away' visits. We get most of our repeat bookings because of the reputation we have developed for the quality of our food and attentive and courteous service.

The Squire Hotel in Oxford has 41 bedrooms and is situated close to Magdalen College. The entrance lobby is small but pleasantly decorated. The room is dominated by a grandfather clock and an elegant mahogany desk. Charles Harper, the hotel's manager, explained:

> I do not like the traditional counter arrangement, I like a simple, open and friendly situation with a clear desk to demonstrate our uncluttered and caring attitude. Even our computers are kept in a small room just off the lobby, out of sight. I want my guests to feel that they are important and not just one of the 70 that we are going to deal with that evening.

SHG's hotel managers are totally responsible for their own operations. They set staff levels and wages within clear guidelines set by head office. Although pricing policy is determined centrally, there is scope for adjustment and they can negotiate with local firms or groups in consultation with head office. Charles Harper added:

> Every year, each hotel manager agrees the financial targets for his own operation with head office, and if the manager does not reach his target without good reason, he may well find himself out of a job. I believe that it is my job to be constantly improving and developing this business. This is naturally reflected in the yearly profit expectations.

The hotel managers report performance to the group monthly on four criteria: occupancy, profit, staff costs and food costs. The information provided allows senior managers to drill down to the costs of individual people and meals. Charles Harper explained:

> My job is to try to get and maintain 100 per cent occupancy rates and keep costs within budget. During the tourist season Oxford has more tourists looking for beds than it has beds, so in the peak season, which is only two months long, we expect to achieve 100 per cent utilisation of rooms. Indeed, I am budgeted for it. This has been a bad year so far. The high value of the pound has kept many American tourists away and our occupancy has sometimes been as low as 90 per cent. In the off-season our occupancy drops to 60 per cent – this is still very good and is due to our excellent location. In the peak season we charge a premium on our rooms. This does not cause any problems, but our guests do expect a high standard of food and service.
>
> We get very few complaints. Usually these are about the food, things like the temperature of the vegetables, though recently we had a complaint from two elderly ladies about the juke-box in the bar. We don't have any formal means of collecting information about quality. Head office may come and check the hotel

once or twice a year. We always know when they are coming and try to look after them. We don't use complaints or suggestion forms in the bedrooms because I think it tends to get people to complain or question the service. However, I do try to collect some information myself in order to get an indication from guests about how they feel about the quality or the price. I don't document the results, but we know what is going on. Our aim is to prevent complaints by asking and acting during the service.

I have 40 staff, most of whom are full-time. Ten work mainly on the liquor side, 20 on food and 10 on apartments. There is a restaurant manager and a bar manager. Staff turnover is 70 per cent, which compares very well with most hotels, where turnover can be as high as 300 per cent. In general the staff are very good and seem to enjoy working here.

The restaurant at the Squire Hotel in Oxford has 20 tables with a total seating capacity of 100. The restaurant is well used at lunchtime by tourists and visitors to the local colleges and by local business people. However, there are several excellent and famous restaurants that tend to draw potential customers and even hotel guests away from the hotel restaurant in the evenings.

The restaurant managers have considerable discretion in menu planning, purchasing and staffing, providing they keep to the budgets set by head office. These budgets specify, for example, the food and staff costs for an individual breakfast, lunch and dinner. Overall food costs and staff costs are reported weekly to the hotel manager. The style of restaurants in the hotels varies considerably from carvery to à la carte, with the decisions made on the basis of the type of hotel and the requirements of the local community. Elizabeth Dickens, the restaurant manager, explained:

My job is concerned with keeping to food and staff budgets, and so most of my time is taken up with staffing, purchasing and menu planning. At lunchtime, for example, I provide four items, three traditional and one vegetarian, and these change weekly. We aim to serve a main course within 15 minutes of taking an order. I am constantly looking for new ideas for our menus and better ways of serving but I am constrained by continually tightening budgets from head office. I think we have now reached the point where we are starting to lose many of our established customers. We really do need to respond to the changing demands of our customers in terms of speed of service, particularly at lunchtimes, and changes in diet together with the desire for a greater and more interesting range of meals. I think head office is out of touch with reality.

Questions

1   Evaluate the performance measures in place at the Squire Hotel Group.

2   What improvements would you suggest?